RAILWAYS OF TASMANIA'S WILD WEST

NICK ANCHEN

Published by Sierra Publishing, Melbourne www.sierraaustralia.com
First edition 2014

Designed by Nick Anchen, with assistance from Andrew Cunningham of Studio Pazzo.

Pre press by Splitting Image Pty Ltd, Melbourne

Printed in China by iBook

National Library of Australia
Cataloguing-in-publication information

Anchen, Nick
Railways of Tasmania's Wild West

First edition
ISBN 978-0-9807640-7-9 (hbk)

Railroads – Tasmania – History
Horse tramways – Tasmania – History
Mines and mineral resources – Tasmania – History
Railroads – Employees – Biography
Mineral industries – Employees – Biography
Tasmania, Western – History

385.09946

WRITTEN REFERENCES

BOOKS

Barrack, Richard and Heerey, Peter, *Railways and Tramways on the West Coast of Tasmania*, Train Hobby Publications, Melbourne, 2009
Blainey, Geoffrey, *The Peaks of Lyell*, Melbourne University Press, Melbourne, 1954
Butrims, Robert, *Australia's Garratt*, Geelong Steam Preservation Society, 1975
Clarke, Marcus, *For the Term of his Natural Life*, Australian Journal, 1874
Cooley, Thomas, *Railroading in Tasmania*, Government Printing Office, Hobart, 1963
Rae, Lou, *The Emu Bay Railway*, self-published, Hobart, 1991
Rae, Lou, *The Abt Railway*, self-published, Hobart, 1994
Railtrails Australia, *Rail Trails of Tasmania*, East Melbourne, 2003

MAGAZINES

Bulletin, Australian Railway Historical Society
Light Railways, Light Railway Research Society of Australia
Tasmanian Rail News, Australian Railway Historical Society Tasmanian Division

NEWSPAPERS

Burnie Advocate
Hobart Mercury
Launceston Enquirer

FRONT COVER: In the wilds of western Tasmania, a train ascends the 1 in 20 rack section of the Mount Lyell Railway, between Dubbil Barril and Rinadeena. The load consists of coke for the Mount Lyell smelter. November 1962. ~ Bernie Kelly

BACK COVER: In November 1962, ASG No.17 blasts over the Pieman River bridge, whilst hauling a Burnie-bound goods train on the Emu Bay Railway. ~ Bernie Kelly

TITLE PAGE: *Wee Georgie Wood* pictured at Tullah mine in the early 1960s.
~ Jim Baines, John Robin collection

ACKNOWLEDGEMENTS

A publication such as this requires the assistance and co-operation of many people and organisations. I sincerely thank you all, and trust the end result was worth the effort. In particular, I am heavily indebted to retired Emu Bay Railway engineman Hedley Charles, along with historian and photographer Peter Ralph, both of whom provided unlimited encouragement throughout the production of this book.

The invaluable proof reading and editorial assistance was ably provided by Emile Badawy, Hedley Charles, Viv & Judy Crocker, Andrew Hennell, David Hennell, and Tony 'Ashcat' Marsden.

A special mention is due to all the photographers represented in these pages, especially Keith Atkinson, Jim Baines, Ray Bruce, Bernie Kelly, Frank Kelly, Weston Langford, Peter Ralph and Michael Schrader. Thank goodness for the foresight of these men, who recorded the fast-disappearing West Coast railway and mining activity before it vanished.

Additonal photographic material was also provided by the Abt Railway Society, Geoff Brown, Lorraine Bugg and Leo Deacon at The Galley Museum in Queenstown, Burnie Regional Museum, Neville Gee of Train Hobby Publications, Images of Yesteryear, Daryl Luke, Tony 'Ashcat' Marsden, John Robin, Neil Tate, James Smith, Phil Vickers and Teena Jones at the West Coast Heritage Centre in Zeehan, and Warren Woodberry of Don River Railway.

Interviews were conducted with former Emu Bay Railway drivers Geoff Brown, Hedley Charles and Daryl Luke; former Mount Lyell employee Viv Crocker; and Tasmanian enthusiast Peter Ralph. Peter Beck's 1998 interview with Viv & Judy Crocker was also utilised. Mark Tregoning generously provided the notes from former Mount Lyell driver Mick Maxfield.

And for assistance in many ways, large and small, all of which contributed to making this publication a reality: Megan Anchen, Mikayla Anchen, Andrew Cunningham at Studio Pazzo, Rod Davies at Splitting Image, former EBR Permanent Way inspector Herbert Illichman, Rob McMurray, former EBR drivers John Watkins and Sid Young, and last but definitely not least, the exceptionally friendly and helpful people at the West Coast Wilderness Railway, in particular Geoff 'Gas' Haines, Allie Hume, Allan Johnstone, Tristan McMahon, Troy O'Mahoney, Geoff Rollins, James Smith and Mark Tregoning.

ABOUT THE AUTHOR

Author and photographer Nick Anchen first ventured into the wilds of western Tasmania in June 2000, and he rapidly became captivated by the fascinating mining heritage and superb scenery to be found. Further adventures followed, which involved detailed exploration of the region's former railways, tramways and mining relics, plus several memorable journeys along the old Emu Bay Railway.

It was these adventures, along with the superb writing of Geoffrey Blainey, Marcus Clarke and Lou Rae, and the interviews conducted with former Emu Bay Railway and Mount Lyell employees, which provided the inspiration to produce this book. *Railways of Tasmania's Wild West* is a tribute to a truly remarkable region, and one of Australia's great mining success stories.

Nick Anchen joined what was left of the Victorian Railways in 1999, becoming a driver on Melbourne's suburban network. His writing and publishing career began in 2007 with the release of his best-selling book *Puffing Billy – Spirit of the Dandenongs*, and this title has been followed by many others.

Nick lives with his family in Ferntree Gully, Victoria.

Other books by Nick Anchen include:

Puffing Billy – Spirit of the Dandenongs
The Cuckoo
The Dandenongs
Railways of the Yarra Valley
The Colour of Australia
Railways of the Otway Ranges
Rails to Old Walhalla
Enginemen of the Victorian Railways
The Narrow Gauge
A Railway to Cudgewa
Life on the Victorian Railways

Photo by Ken Coram

RAILWAYS OF TASMANIA'S WILD WEST

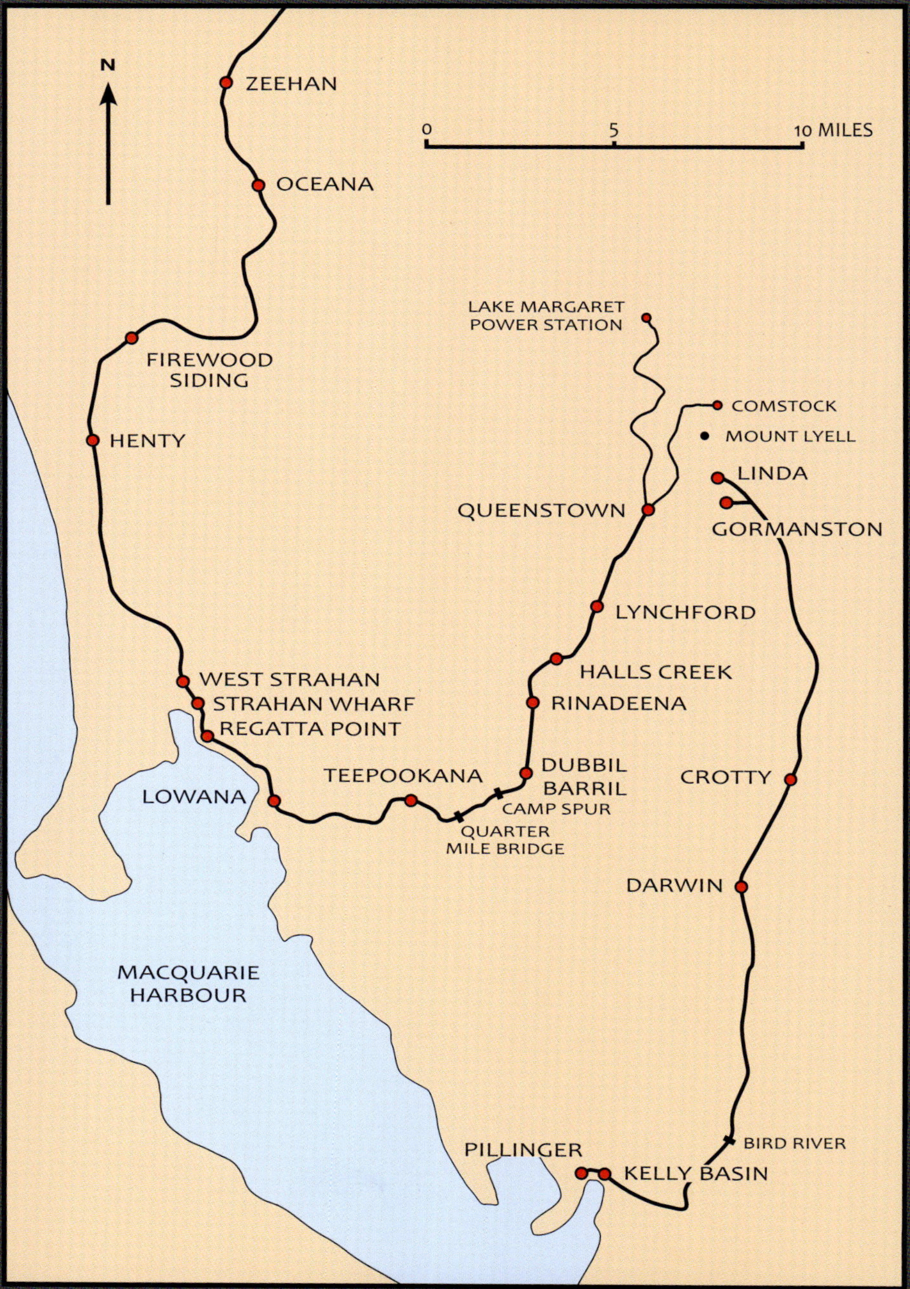

BASS STRAIT
EMU BAY
BURNIE
PIGEON HILL
RIDGLEY
HIGHCLERE
TASMANIA
HAMPSHIRE
RINGWOOD
TORONNA
MOUNT BISCHOFF
GUILDFORD JUNCTION
MAGNET
WARATAH
MOORY JUNCTION
HATFIELD
HELLYER MINE
QUE HILL
BULGOBAC
BOCO (ALSO KNOWN AS BOKO)
FARRELL JUNCTION
PIEMAN RIVER
TULLAH
N
BOBADIL BANK
RING RIVER
PRIMROSE
ROSEBERY
RENISON BELL
ARGENT TUNNEL
WILLIAMSFORD
HERCULES HAULAGE
MELBA FLATS
MONTEZUMA FALLS
RAYNA JUNCTION
DUNDAS
MAESTRIS
ZEEHAN
0 10 20 MILES

N
ZEEHAN
0 5 10 MILES
OCEANA
LAKE MARGARET POWER STATION
FIREWOOD SIDING
COMSTOCK
MOUNT LYELL
HENTY
LINDA
QUEENSTOWN
GORMANSTON
LYNCHFORD
HALLS CREEK
WEST STRAHAN
STRAHAN WHARF
RINADEENA
REGATTA POINT
TEEPOOKANA
DUBBIL BARRIL
CROTTY
LOWANA
CAMP SPUR
QUARTER MILE BRIDGE
DARWIN
MACQUARIE HARBOUR
PILLINGER
BIRD RIVER
KELLY BASIN

CONTENTS

Riley inspection car at Regatta Point on the Mount Lyell Railway. July 1963. ~ Michael Schrader, Train Hobby Publications

TASMANIA'S WILD WEST

The first known European sighting of Tasmania's wild West Coast occurred in 1642, when Dutch explorer Abel Janszoon Tasman sailed from Batavia on a voyage of discovery. His ships, named *Zeehan* and *Heemskerck*, sailed around the southern portion of this previously unknown land, and upon reaching the East Coast, Tasman claimed the new territory for Holland. He named it Van Diemenslandt, in honour of the Governor-General of the Dutch East Indies, Anthony van Diemen. While sailing near the West Coast, Tasman noted in his journal the erratic behaviour of his ship's compass, which was thought to be caused by the existence of magnetite, or loadstone. This observation was to prove accurate, as the mountains in this rain-soaked wilderness contained one of the world's great treasure troves of mineral wealth.

In 1798, British sailors George Bass and Matthew Flinders discovered that the mysterious landmass was in fact an island, and in 1803 Van Diemen's Land was officially claimed as part of the Colony of New South Wales.

On the East Coast at Port Arthur, a penal colony was established, and the new territory surrounding the rapidly growing Hobart Town attracted squatters and other free settlers.

The coastline of Van Diemen's Land was circumnavigated in 1815 by James Kelly, and during this adventure through raging seas and shattering surf, a waterway named Macquarie Harbour was discovered. This notorious, brooding body of water, with its treacherous entrance later known as 'Hell's Gate', was selected as another penal settlement – Sarah Island – reserved for the 'incorrigibles', the hardened and most difficult convicts. This despised, loathsome establishment operated only from 1822 to 1833, but with horrifying stories of brutality, escape attempts and cannibal convicts, this living 'hell-on-earth' attained a fearsome reputation. After the abandonment of Sarah Island, the untamed wilderness became the domain of the timber-getters, who battled the almost impenetrable, rain-soaked forests in search of Huon Pine.

The relentless, pounding surf of Tasmania's wild West Coast. ~ Nick Anchen

Majestic Bird River wilderness, near Macquarie Harbour. ~ Nick Anchen

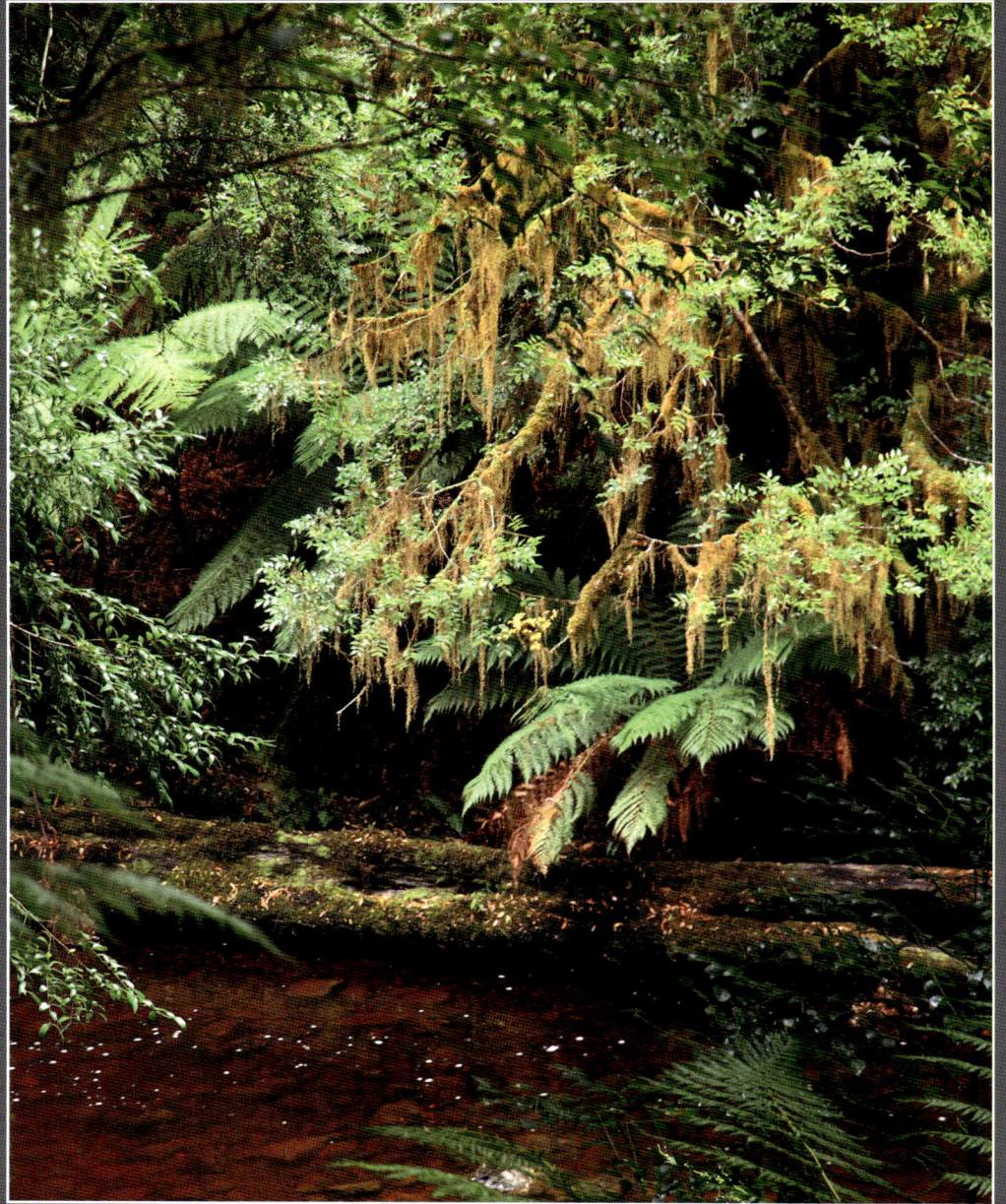

Tasmanian rainforest magnificence. ~ All images Nick Anchen

During the 1850s and 1860s, prospectors began searching for minerals, and sporadic discoveries were made, but these were overshadowed by the stupendous gold rushes to the north of Bass Strait, in Victoria and New South Wales. Then in 1871, a promising discovery occurred at a remote location some 30 miles south of the settlement at Emu Bay, on the island's North Coast. It was a virtual mountain of tin, and was destined to become the most successful tin mine in the world – Mount Bischoff. This discovery was followed by many others, the most significant being at Mount Lyell, which became a fabulously rich source of copper. Before long, the West Coast of Tasmania – as the colony had been re-named in 1856 – was regarded as one of the most exciting fields of mineral wealth in the British Empire.

The treacherous weather conditions experienced along Tasmania's coastline wreaked havoc on ships attempting to ply its perilous waterways, and this problem influenced the future of transport. The port at Emu Bay, on the North Coast, was considered a superior option to that of Macquarie Harbour, where ships occasionally waited weeks to gain entry, and this resulted in the town of Burnie becoming a focal point for railway builders. Affordable transport was a crucial factor in the success or failure of any mining venture, and the tremendous effort – not to mention expense – in pushing the narrow gauge railways and tramways through such rugged country speaks volumes for the expected value and quantity of the ore being mined. The motto of the former Mount Lyell Mining and Railway Company said it all: Labor Omnia Vincit – 'We Find a Way or Make It'.

During the heyday of mining activities, Tasmania's West Coast was isolated from the rest of the state. The first proper road from Hobart reached Queenstown only in 1932, and it was not until 1963 that the completion of the Murchison Highway provided access to Burnie and the North Coast. This isolation resulted in a great reliance – and in turn great affection – for the railways and scores of tramways which snaked their way through the mountains, and became the lifeblood for isolated mountain town such as Tullah and Queenstown. These iron roads in the wilderness necessitated remarkable engineering feats, and one can only admire the bravery and endurance of the surveyors, the engineers, and particularly the construction teams who, by sheer determination, cleared the seemingly impenetrable rainforest, dug the cuttings, erected the bridges and laid the rails, all the while battling the most rugged terrain and worst weather conditions to be found in Australia.

The hardships that these pioneers faced can scarcely be imagined in today's modern world. Mining continues into the 21st century, with modern methods and mechanisation having greatly reduced the hazards and backbreaking effort of the old days. To visit the region today, a great deal of imagination is required to picture the scenes from the old days, when the mountains and valleys were alive with mines and men, railways and tramways, timber cutters and rough settlements hacked out of the bush, all with a single purpose – to extract the precious metals which would make men rich.

Mallet articulated locomotive on the 2 ft gauge Magnet Tramway. Early 1900s. ~ Images of Yesteryear

EMU BAY RAILWAY

Australian Standard Garratt locomotive No. 20A takes water at the 62 mile tank, between Boco and Farrell. 28 January 1963. ~ Weston Langford

The Emu Bay Railway, that venerable iron road of Tasmania's rugged north west, is one of the great stories in Australian railway history. This spectacular 88 mile, 3 ft 6 in gauge line – most of which remains in operation today – is one of the few survivors from the plethora of railways and tramways which once criss-crossed the area.

The ERB's history mirrored the fortunes of the mining companies for which it was built, and was likewise vulnerable to the same external pressures. That the company survived for over a century, withstanding wildly fluctuating metal prices, two World Wars, the Great Depression and the erratic wrath of Mother Nature, speaks volumes about the dedication of its management and staff.

The EBR began life in 1878 as a 45 mile horse-drawn tramway, of 3 ft gauge with wooden rails. The line was constructed by the Van Diemen's Land Company to connect the spectacularly successful Mount Bischoff tin mine near Waratah to the port of Emu Bay, later called Burnie. By 1884, the tramway had been upgraded and re-laid with iron rails, becoming a proper steam hauled 3 ft 6 in gauge railway.

EBR construction workers, building the line the hard way.
~ Burnie Regional Museum

Emu Bay and Mount Bischoff Railway.

ORDINARY TRAIN SERVICE TIME TABLE.

COMMENCING 1st MARCH 1885.

DOWN				UP			
Mileage.	Stations	Arrive	Depart	Mileage	Stations	Arrive	Depart
		A. M.	A. M.			P. M.	P. M.
0	Emu Bay		8	0	Waratah		2
4	Four Mile	8.15		8	Hellyer	2.25	2.33
7	Pigeon Hill	8.26	8.34	12	Surrey Hills	2.48	
10	Ridgley	8.45		15	Wey	2.59	
12	Highclere	8.53		18	Broadlands	3.10	
20	Hampshire	9.23	9.33	25	Ringwood	3.36	3.40
23	Ringwood	9.44	9.48	28	Hampshire	3.52	3.57
30	Broadlands	10.16		36	Highclere	4.27	
33	Wey	10.27		38	Ridgley	4.35	
36	Surrey Hills	10.39		41	Pigeon Hill	4.47	4.59
40	Hellyer	10.54	11.2	44	Four Mile	5.11	
48	Waratah	11.30		48	Emu Bay	5.30	

J. W. NORTON-SMITH, Manager.

W. W. Smithies, Printer, Leven.

Stylish 1885 Emu Bay and Mount Bischoff Railway timetable.
~ Burnie Regional Museum

The Mount Bischoff tin mine was one of the great chapters in the rich annals of West Coast mining history. James 'Philosopher' Smith had discovered tin in exciting quantities in 1871, and within a few years the mine became one of the most productive in the world. When it was finally closed in 1947, it had produced a phenomenal 56,000 tons of tin, rewarding its shareholders with a stupendous £2,225,000 in dividends.

In 1897, the Emu Bay Railway Company was formed and took over operations from the VDLC. Meanwhile, in the Mount Lyell field to the south, copper was being extracted in remarkable quantities. The excitement generated by the Mount Lyell field resulted in a series of extravagant and fanciful railway construction proposals, in a period which became known as the West Coast Railway War. The proposals included an electrified line from Hobart, to be called the Great Western Railway, but the cost estimates were enormous and the idea foundered.

Burnie railway station, c.1900. ~ Burnie Regional Museum

The EBR wasted little time extending its line south from Guildford in the direction of Mount Lyell, with the rails reaching Rosebery in 1899. Other than heavy earthworks, the main engineering difficulty along this 33 mile section was the crossing of Pieman River, which was spanned by a 200 ft long steel lattice bridge. Final positioning of this heavy bridge proved to be a dangerous exercise, with three men being killed during the process.

Soon, construction of the final seventeen miles to Zeehan commenced. This section required a number of bridges, including substantial structures crossing the Stitt and Ring Rivers, along with the boring of the ¼ mile-long Argent tunnel, which took eighteen months to build at a cost of £30,000. The railhead advanced steadily, with the arrival of the first official train at Zeehan on 21 December 1900 being celebrated with gusto.

ENGINEERING EXCELLENCE

Upon completion, the Emu Bay Railway was a magnificent engineering achievement, and a line of scenic splendour. The 88 miles of narrow gauge track rounded tortuous curves, negotiated steep gradients, passed through deep cuttings and crossed high embankments, skirted mountain ranges, plunged into dark, jungle-like forests, crossed button grass alpine meadows and windswept plains and spanned raging rivers on tall bridges. All this in a region of Tasmania which receives occasional heavy snowfalls, along with quite spectacular rainfall, with Rosebery averaging over 86 inches per year.

The railway became a lifeline for the remote mountain communities to which it was connected, replacing the muddy, often impassable tracks which had previously served as roads. Traffic on the EBR was substantially bolstered by the numerous feeder tramways which ran from the bush. These included the Magnet Tramway at Waratah and the North Mount Farrell Tramway, which connected initially at Boco, then later at Farrell. Upon opening to Zeehan, trains ran six days per week. Other than mining company supplies, timber and ore concentrates, the railway carted all the necessities of life including the mail, groceries and livestock, along with a healthy number of passengers, in the period before efficient road transport was able to compete. Summertime picnic trains were also a very popular feature of the EBR in the early days.

EBR's 0-6-4 Neilson locomotive crossing the substantial iron bridge at Waratah. ~ Burnie Regional Museum

Dübs No. 6 bursts out of Argent tunnel whilst hauling the No.11 Mail train from Zeehan to Burnie. 1937. ~ Burnie Regional Museum

Rail Motor No. 1, a 30 hp AEC, at Waratah in 1925. The EBR manager, James Stirling, is at far left with pipe in hand. ~ Burnie Regional Museum

The Ring River bridge was washed away by raging floodwaters in March 1917.
~ Geoff Brown collection

Oops! Dübs loco derailed near Burnie. 1930s. ~ Burnie Regional Museum

Dübs loco on the rebuilt Ring River bridge. September 1917.
~ Geoff Brown collection

MOUNT BISCHOFF MINE TRAMWAY

The Mount Bischoff tin mine was situated 1¼ miles from the town of Waratah, and a tramway was built to transport ore from the mine to the dressing sheds in town. From here, the refined product was transhipped to Emu Bay Railway wagons and then railed to Burnie. This tramway was built in 1875 and was horse-drawn with wooden rails. In 1881, the line was converted to steam powered 3 ft gauge. Then in 1907, the company electrified the tramway, operating it with a Westinghouse Electric locomotive. The mine and tramway closed in 1929, although limited mining operations continued until 1947.

MAGNET TRAM

In 1901, a ten mile 2 ft gauge line was built from Magnet Junction, a point on the EBR near Waratah, to the silver mining town of Magnet. Two Orenstein & Koeppel 0-4-4-0 Mallet locomotives, along with an 0-6-0 Orenstein & Koppel loco, provided the motive power for the tramway. It was substantially built, with steel rails and numerous curves, and a maximum gradient of 1 in 25, which allowed loads of up to 35 tons. The Magnet mine had opened in 1894, and operated productively until effectively closing in 1932, although work spluttered on until 1940.

LEFT: Mallet locomotive No. 2 of the Magnet Silver Mining Company's 2 ft gauge tramway, taking water whilst hauling a trainload of eager-looking passengers. ~ Burnie Regional Museum

BELOW: Mallet locomotive at Magnet. ~ West Coast Pioneer's Museum, Zeehan

Emu Bay Railway Ganger 1937-1948

Archie Radford

EBR fettlers on Que Hill, after a heavy snowfall in the late 1940s. ~ Burnie Regional Museum

Archie Radford's memories of his time with the EBR, written in 1996 at the age of 81, provide a fascinating glimpse into another world. With high unemployment following the Great Depression, men took whatever jobs were on offer, often finding themselves working in harsh, isolated conditions, with low pay and few creature comforts.

SLEEPER CUTTING

In 1936, the worst depression the world had known was almost over, and we were on the threshold of better times. I was living at Highclere with my mother and father, and worked for various farmers around the district for the wage of eight shillings per day – the usual wage for farm labourers at the time.

The mining town of Rosebery had been waiting for the Great Depression to end, and their mining operations were about to start up again. By this time the Emu Bay Railway had acquired their big Garratt engines to haul the minerals to Burnie, and after they'd been in operation for a few months, management realised that the track needed upgrading. Railway sleepers were required, and quickly. Before long, farmers' sons from the Highclere and Ridgley areas, armed with axes and saws, were on their way to the West Coast.

Bulgobac was our stopping place, as celery pine, which produced a good sleeper, was readily available there. I worked with my two brothers, Wilfred and Leighton. After a week of much frustration, coping with leeches and a few snakes, and battling horizontal scrub, we were starting to make progress cutting celery pine. These had the nasty habit of growing in the thickest part of the wild vegetation, and quite a lot of clearing had to be done before a tree could be felled. They were not big trees – the largest being no more than 2 foot 6 inches in diameter – but they grew very tall and had only a few branches at the top. After the first week of learning, we set our target at sixteen sleepers a piece per day, and after some weeks we could achieve this easily. We received one shilling and threepence per sleeper, and the man pulling them out of the bush to the railway line received one shilling per sleeper.

EBR FETTLER

We worked at this job for some months, and when the pine became scarcer we were offered a job as fettlers on the EBR, based at Bulgobac. We took up the offer, and started work in January 1937. The wage was about twelve shillings per day, plus free travel on the train, so we came home to Highclere at the end of every fortnight. The section of line we looked after was seven miles north towards Guildford, which included the treacherous Que Hill, and three miles south from Bulgobac to the 59 mile point. This section had a 1½ mile straight – the longest straight on the entire EBR. Evard Allen was my boss and there were six of us in the gang. Our main job was putting new sleepers in the track. We soon adapted to the work and it was quite a good job.

My two brothers left after about nine months and went to work, still at Bulgobac, for Jack Fidler who had the contract to supply timber for the Rosebery mine. They were bushmen and they liked working in the bush. Mr. Allen left the job a few months later and another boss was sent to us, a man named Stan Pitham. He could not come to terms with batching and cooking for himself and he became very frustrated about it. In our gang was a chap who had a girlfriend in Rosebery, and he went there every weekend to see her. We were only entitled to go out every fortnight, so he and Pitham had quite a few arguments about the matter, and in the end it came to fisticuffs! The fettler was sacked, and Pitham returned to the Guildford gang. Mr. Roy Wills, the EBR inspector, came down the next day to interview us. He said to me, 'I haven't got a replacement boss, so I'm putting you in charge until I find someone to do the job.' We worked on for about a month and then he came through and told me that my position as Ganger was permanent.

EBR GANGER

At 24, I was the second youngest ganger the EBR had ever appointed. My first job was to re-sleeper the long straight towards Rosebery. A mile and a half section had lots of sleepers, but we got through. Extra men were sent down from Waratah, so now I had ten men to look after. I found that some of these Waratah men were more interested in drinking beer than working, but I soon sorted them out and they got the message loud and clear. I made one lifelong friend out of these men, Jack Wells.

By now it was 1939, and war was looming, with the 3rd of September being that dreadful day. The manager, Fred McCormack and the Inspector, Roy Wills, came through soon after the war had started. I said to them, 'What is the situation as far as me joining the army?' Fred said, 'Forget about it – your job is here.' He said that the company had three married gangers and married men simply wouldn't stop at Bulgobac, so it was more essential than ever that we maintain the line to get the metal out of Rosebery. So I was tied down to essential services for the duration of the war.

Dübs locomotive in heavy snow near Hatfield. ~ Burnie Regional Museum

LIFE AT BULGOBAC

In the early 1940s the line to Waratah was closed down and pulled up. The Waratah station building was brought down to Bulgobac and rebuilt as a camp for us fettlers. It had four rooms, was lined with weatherboard and pine, and four of us camped in it. It was quite comfortable, and a great improvement over the tent in which I'd been living for almost three years. They even provided us with a tank for our drinking water, so we no longer had to carry water from the creek. We had very limited recreation. We knocked off at four o'clock in the afternoon, and as we were coming home we would stop and fall a few saplings, which we'd cart home and then entertain ourselves with a small chopping carnival. In the early 1940s I trained my brother for the Rosebery carnival, where he won the chop easily, and in later years went on to be a very good axeman. Several years later I also won the Rosebery carnival. At night we usually played cards – 500 was the most popular game, and then it was early to bed to be ready for the seven o'clock start.

We had to patrol our section of seven miles towards Guildford every day – regardless of the weather! Trees and rocks often came down overnight, and we found quite a few that could have derailed a train. If it snowed, we had to walk it, and believe you me, walking seven miles in about a foot of snow is no easy task. We had 2¼ hours to do it, as the Garratt from Burnie would be on our section by about 9.15 am. The train would stop to pick us up, and we'd ride back to wherever the rest of the gang were.

A fettler and his wife, George and Eva Luke, lived at Bulgobac. George patrolled the three miles towards Rosebery each morning before joining his own gang, and Eva ran the post office for us. Their son, Daryl, later went on to become an EBR driver. Eva was a wonderfully kind person who was always ready to help a bushman or fettler who had been injured.

The weather on the west coast was one of two extremes – lovely in summer but atrocious in winter. Three or four months of summer, then April to June was frosts and the start of winter. In the first year when I was a fettler we had 35 frosts straight without a break. Bulgobac was a watering place for trains, and there was a pipeline running from half a mile up in the bush to the tank. Two inch pipes were used, and during that frosty period the whole pipeline became frozen. We had to undo every section of pipe and run each of them through a fire to clear them and then join them up again – a task which took three days. We had heavy falls of snow from July to October. In those days the telephone line followed the railway all the way to the west coast towns, and sometimes the snow built up on the telephone wire until it broke under the weight.

During the summer months we worked as much as we could on the Que Hill, keeping the track in order and keeping the cuttings clear of bushes and small trees – as the snow in winter would bend the trees over the line and obscure the vision of the train drivers. The drains and culverts had to be cleaned ready for winter, too. Summertime caused a few problems for us, as the rails expanded in the heat, making the curves 'thick out' and go out of alignment. We only had two hours between trains coming and going, and in that time we had to cut both rails and get them back into alignment. We only had a hacksaw to do this job, a far cry from the torches used today. Due to the soft nature of the railway foundation we had lots of trouble with some curves – where the lower rail would sink and put too much elevation on the curve. 2½ inches was the correct elevation for a five chain curve, and when it got beyond that we had to lift the lower rail and repack it. The section between Que Filling – a filled in bridge – and Que Farm was the hardest for us to look after, and these troubles persist to this day.

Life on the railway continued from one year to the next and was much the same as any other job. Our job was simply to keep the trains running. The years went by, the war ended, and new rails were available. On our section we got enough to renew from 52 mile to 54 mile. The new rails were 45 feet long and 60 lb to the yard, and were a great improvement on the old 24 ft length 40 lb rails which they replaced.

As in all jobs, pay day was eagerly looked forward to, and this was on every second Wednesday. Edgar Threthewey was our pay master and Stan Dumphy assisted him. They travelled in a first class carriage attached to a goods train. Escorted to the train under strict security, they began their trip at Burnie, then stopped where every gang was working and handed out the pay. Each man had a token brass tag about the size of a ten cent piece with a number on it, and as the paymaster called the number out, the worker handed over his token.

Our working conditions were pretty tough, but I had lots of good workmates in my time, along with a few roughies. Most of us got on well together and we did the job to the best of our ability. The last gang I had were good, hardworking and loyal fellows, all of whom are now deceased. Their names were Edgar 'Nip' Twining, Alan Hayward, Alfie Hayward and Len Molan. The gangers whom I knew in my day were Gordon Little at Zeehan, George Luke at Bulgobac, Billy Hampton at Rosebery, Gordon Summers, Charlie Wilson and Mac Ansell at Guildford, Monty Smith at Highclere, Jim Ansell and Lennie Cummings at Burnie.

Drivers in my time were Norm and Wilf Summers, Cyril Butt, Alma Clark, Jack Wilson, Ingram Cartledge, Jim Tobin, Hilton Sharpe, Jim and Dick Norton-Smith, Reg Flight, Roy and Syd Townsend, Cecil Lunson and George Gittens. Guards were Andy Ingles, Viv Mott, Lindsay Wilson, Mick Lucas, Walter 'Watty' Kidd, Bert Adams, Harold 'Fatty' Burgess and Frank Reid.

I left the EBR in 1948. Although the company was always good to me and I was grateful to the management and staff, I always longed to be a farmer and that was my next assignment. But that is another story!

Beyer Garratt No. 12 taking water at the 32 mile tank, while running a southbound train in the 1950s.
~ John Watkins, Burnie Regional Museum

LIFE ON THE EMU BAY RAILWAY

HEDLEY CHARLES

Hedley Charles began his 44 year career with the Emu Bay Railway in 1954, as a blacksmith's labourer. He then progressed through the ranks from cleaner to fireman, then driver, working on all the steam and diesel locomotives of the period, before taking on the role of traffic controller.

When Hedley retired in 1998, shortly after the company's centenary celebrations, it was the end of an era – he was the last of the steam men still on the job. Following retirement, Hedley has become a respected EBR historian – the custodian of a wealth of information – and his memories paint a fascinating picture of life on the Emu Bay Railway.

A 44 YEAR CAREER

I was born in 1937, the fifth of seven children, and my family lived on a farm at West Ridgley, thirteen miles south of Burnie. My first memories of steam trains were of hearing them running on the Emu Bay Railway, which was only about five miles from where we were living. As a ten year old child, I often had the morning task of hooking up a horse and jinker and taking out boxes of freshly caught rabbit carcasses to the nearest railway siding, which was at Highclere. From here, they would be loaded onto the train and travel down the West Coast to Zeehan or Queenstown.

West Ridgley school was the proverbial one teacher school, and we walked 3½ miles to get there each day. One of our early teachers was a very stern Irishman, and a little verse which he instilled in us was 'Hail, rain or snow, it's school we love to go.' After walking the 3½ miles through rain and snow, it was indeed wonderful to get to school with its open fire! Being part of a big family on a farm, I learned at a very young age about chasing cows around and digging spuds and so on. As a young bloke I took jobs around the district such as stacking hay and falling trees out in the bush, and also splitting posts, rails and palings, but I didn't see much of a future on the farm. Hydro electric power had not yet reached our house, and consequently it was all kerosene lamps and candles. Our main source of entertainment was the radio, to which we listened constantly. This ran off car batteries or dry cell batteries. Mum was bed-ridden with multiple sclerosis, so by the time I was ten years old I found myself chief cook and bottle washer.

I commenced working for the Emu Bay Railway on 25 October 1954. There were four blacksmiths employed on the railway at the time, and I started work as a blacksmith's labourer, or a 'blacksmith's striker', to be more precise – an occupation which no longer exists. This work involved operating a forge and an air powered hammer, and it was very heavy work. We made tools such as hammers and spanners, and we repaired locomotive parts such as connecting rods. We also made springs and spring hangers, and things such as dog spikes. I had about twelve months in the blacksmith's shop, during which time I helped re-tube an entire ASG locomotive boiler, and it was not uncommon to do ten or twelve hour shifts – my introduction to shift work.

ASG 17 in the Burnie shed. ~ Rolf Frank, Train Hobby Publications

ENGINE CLEANING

My mode of transport during my early days on the EBR was a motorbike, and I was the proud owner of an Ariel 500. I was still living at home up at West Ridgley, before I got a place in Burnie to live in, so I had to get a licence. I went down to see the copper at Burnie. He said, 'Well that won't be a problem – I've seen you riding around plenty of times. I thought you must have already had a licence! He told me to ride around the streets, and when I came back he said, 'Well, how'd you go?' I said, 'All right', and he wrote out the licence!

On my first day as a cleaner it was a very frosty morning. I left home at an early hour and crossed the wooden bridge over the Guide River, but as soon as I hit the frost and touched the throttle, down she went. Not only did I fall off, but the motorbike chain snapped as well. I was about to begin walking to Ridgley to call work and tell them that I'd broken down, when an old bloke came along in a ute. He said he was going to Burnie, and he'd take me there, so after I got the bike to a repair shop and made my way to work, it was about lunch time. My first pay as an engine cleaner was half wiped out on motorcycle repairs!

Two of the other cleaners also had motorcycles, both Triumph twins. The three of us were working in the shed one Easter, and after we'd finished our cleaning on afternoon shift, we brought our bikes into the shed to clean them. We used to spray the bikes with phenyle, and then use the high pressure hose. On this particular night, near midnight, my mate started his bike up and rode it up and down the shed. The nightshift driver wasn't aware of our bike cleaning ritual, and he said, 'What the hell are you doing?' 'We're cleaning our bikes', I said. He replied 'You're not here to clean motorbikes – you're here to clean locos. I've got a good mind to dob you in!' I said, 'Oh come on, we've finished our work', as a young fellow would. So we weren't very popular with him for a while.

The pay wasn't great as a cleaner. We worked an eight hour day, and there were always about two or three of us on at any given time, day or night. There was a fair turnover of young cleaners in my time, as it was a hard, dirty job, although I soon got used to it. Many young fellows started and only lasted a few months before throwing it in.

I began learning the ropes as a trainee fireman, which meant being put on the shunting engine at Burnie. The shunting engines were Martin 2-6-0s, Nos. 4, 5 and 9. They never left Burnie yard, except when they were put on what we called a 'cinder run', where we took anything up to half a dozen wagons full of cinders several miles out and dumped them by the side of the track. I had just on twelve months of cleaning duties before I went out firing in late 1956.

RIGHT: One of the EBR's 2-6-0 Martin locomotives at Burnie. Note Fordson rail tractor in the background. ~ Burnie Regional Museum

FIRING DAYS

Whilst cleaning was a dirty job, firing was a hard job, but I was used to that – we were brought up on hard work. I really enjoyed my time as a fireman, I found it a great pleasure to work on the steam engines. In those days, when you went out firing, you also went out as a travelling mechanic with the driver. The drivers had to pass pretty rigid exams, as once you went out on the track you were on your own. The line ran mostly through a wilderness area with no road access for the biggest part. If you had trouble you couldn't just get on the nearest phone and say, 'Oh we've broken down, can you send along someone from the workshop to fix us up?'

A trip on the EBR was always a long day, and was always an adventure. Immediately upon leaving Burnie, the line began to climb steeply, and this grade made hard work for the fireman. Our first stop was at a place called Pigeon Hill, where we'd stop twice a week to pick up trucks of livestock – usually sheep – and these would be railed through to Queenstown. The next stop was at Ridgley, about ten miles from Burnie, and this was a watering stop. Highclere was next, which had a passing loop, where we occasionally left trucks, or picked up trucks of potatoes or other produce for the west coast – everything went by rail in those days. The next stop was at Hampshire, which had a crossing loop, and here we used to load pulpwood for the pulp mill at Burnie. Then we used to stop and take on water further up at a place called the 32 mile tank, prior to Guildford.

Guildford had previously been the junction of the branch line which ran out to Waratah, but this branch was shut in 1940, long before I'd started. Guildford had a large station yard with four tracks, and a lot of pulpwood was loaded here for the Burnie mill, as well as logs. It was quite a busy place in its day, and it had justifiably famous refreshment rooms. When you were coming home, it was traditional for the engine crew to water the loco, then pop into the refresh for a quick drink before heading off for Burnie. The Murchison Highway was only opened in 1963, so previous to this, everything travelled down the west coast by rail. When the tourism industry was in its infancy, cars and Pioneer Clipper coaches were carried on the trains, being loaded at Guildford and unloaded at Rosebery. From Guildford we headed off through virgin rainforest country, and now you were heading towards the 'real' west coast. This was mostly myrtle forest, with some hardwood, and the bush was usually very wet. The next location was Hatfield Siding, which was purely a passing loop. Then you headed down what was called Que Hill and passed over the Que River, with the next stop at a little place called Bulgobac where we took water. There was a working sawmill located here when I was firing on the line, and they kept horses which were used to haul logs in from the bush on little trolleys. It was a very primitive way of doing it, but it was quite effective. Logs were sometimes hauled up from Zeehan to Bulgobac, where they were cut up and then taken down to Rosebery to be used as mining timber.

The next station was Boco, where you often crossed all types of trains. Then we headed down what was known as the Boco Hill to Farrell. The tramway to Tullah, with the *Wee Georgie Wood* engine, branched off from here. Farrell was a hard place to start a northbound train from, because it was situated halfway up a 1 in 40 grade. When you had to stop here to pick up loaded wagons from the siding, you'd cut off, pick up the wagons, then reverse back onto the train, and then you had to start on this grade with a full load – a pretty hard thing to ask of any loco driver. This was made even worse if you had been shunting for a while, because the loco got cold and you lost superheated steam.

From Farrell you rolled down and crossed the Pieman River. Then there was quite a steep climb until you reached the top of the grade and ran into Primrose yard. This was the siding for the EZ, the Electolytic Zinc Company of Australasia. Next stop was Rosebery, where the road vehicles were unloaded. The line then ran downhill to the Ring River, and further on there was a tin mine at Renison Bell. A water tank was located prior to the ¼ mile-long Argent tunnel, which was built in 1900. This tunnel had an uphill gradient in the Down direction, so you had to steam all the way through. It was very wet inside the tunnel – it was one place you could guarantee water no matter what the time of year. From here we passed along a straight section of line, which in later years had a loading facility named Melba Flats built on it, from where Mount Lyell copper was loaded. Finally the line ran through to Zeehan.

The main challenge coming home with loaded trains was the short climb after leaving Primrose up what was known as the Bobadil. This was always difficult as you were still running on saturated steam, superheated steam not being available until the loco warmed up. This section had tight curves and was often very greasy due to the steep cuttings. Then there was the climb from Pieman River up to Boco, with its 1 in 40 gradients. After taking water at Bulgobac, engine crews faced another 1 in 40 gradient up the Que hill. These sections were really hard work.

ON THE GARRATTS

The EBR operated three Beyer Garratt locomotives from the 1930s, and they were allowed to haul seven loaded Z wagons, which weighed 42 tons each when fully loaded with ore. Therefore Beyer Garratt loads, including the guard's van, often weighed over 300 tons. As the Beyers began to wear out, there were always two firemen rostered on the footplate. This was because you'd shovel up to twelve tons of coal per trip, and to make things worse we often had trouble with the fire bars clogging up, so it was simply too much for one man. You did at least a twelve hour day on the Beyers, and that was on a good day – if things went wrong, twelve hours could easily extend to fourteen or even sixteen hours.

The EBR also obtained four of the Australian Standard Garratt locos, the ASGs. The ASGs were designed by the Chief Mechanical Engineer of the Western Australian Railways, who himself had come from Armstrong Whitworth in England, and had very close contacts with Beyer Peacock. The ASGs were built during the war, and they had their similarities to the Beyers, but they had a much lighter frame. Our ASGs were ex-Queensland locos, and they were obtained to supplement the ageing loco fleet, which included the Beyers and the smaller Dübs locos. The ASGs were very unpopular with Western Australian and Queensland crews, but the EBR did a lot of modifications and made them a far better engine. These modifications included altering the position of the regulator and the sand gear. They also altered the injectors and strengthened the frames. The firebox door entrance was changed, making it much easier to operate. The wheel alignment was altered, and the leading driving wheels, which were originally flangeless, had wheel flanges added. They were susceptible to cylinder failures due to carrying excess water, and now and then one of them had a piston head smash the end out of its cylinder, which made for a few hours of heavy work for the fitters.

You used about ten tons of coal on the ASGs, meaning only the one fireman was needed, as opposed to two on the Beyers. They started off hauling five of the Z wagons, but as we made such good time with them, management decided to try six! That slowed them down a bit. I loved the ASGs, and preferred them over the Beyers. They weren't quite as strong, but they were superior steamers and they rode beautifully – it was like riding in an armchair at the line's speed of 25 mph – and they were great to fire and drive. The ASGs didn't give us all that much trouble, except when the boiler tubes started leaking.

Loco ASG No. 20 was derailed near Burnie on 20 February 1962, the same night as John Glenn became the first American to orbit the Earth. I stayed up till after midnight to hear about this on the radio, and even though the railway line was only about a mile from my house, I never heard a thing, and only found out about the accident early the next morning. The train came to grief just below the Brooklyn Road crossing, so they only had one more curve to go before they reached Burnie yard. The engine was a write-off, and was replaced with another ASG. I was rostered to drive this loco the following morning, too!

The Garratts burnt a mixture of about 60% Tasmanian coal and 40% Newcastle coal, as there was a heavy ash content in the native coal. Engine crews only worked three days per week on the Garratts, on account of the very long shifts.

DÜBS

I only did a few shifts on the Dübs engines, and they were bloody hard work. I always found them to be hungry for water and coal, as they were working at full capacity and were very unforgiving. They had a long firebox, and you had to learn to fire them a certain way or you'd get into trouble. The drivers seemed to get used to the Dübs, although they were very basic and rough riding and had no comfort at all – just a very hard seat.

In later years Dübs Nos. 6 and 8 were converted to oil firing and were used mainly on the passenger runs, on what was called the *West Coaster* passenger train. They were painted two-tone blue to match this train. The speed recorders were removed from the Dübs when they ran passenger trains, as they were expected to keep to the rail motor's timetable, while still having to take water and so on. The *West Coaster* wasn't a particularly luxurious train, and had no onboard catering whatsoever. It relied on the Guildford refreshment rooms, at which it would stop for about twenty minutes. The train was used by locals and also by the tourist traffic which was increasing on the west coast. On the very last steam hauled *West Coaster* run, the loco ran out of oil on the way back to Burnie, and was rather ingloriously towed back by an ASG. From then on, the train was run by the 10 class diesels.

PAGES 22&23: Beyer Garratt No. 12 gleams in morning sunshine at Hampshire, en route to Primrose. The driver with oil can in hand is Jim Tobin. October 1962. ~ Bernie Kelly

12
C

Beyer Garratt No. 12 taking water at Ridgley tank, en route to Primrose. November 1962.
~ Bernie Kelly

A NIGHTMARE RUN

One day in the early 1960s, after I'd been qualified to drive, John Watkins and I were firing a Beyer Garratt together. The driver was Ray Claridge, who was known to us as 'Unc'. He was a bit of a hard character. Ray was oiling the Beyer this morning at the 32 mile tank, prior to the Wey River, when he fell down between the cowcatcher and the buffers, injuring his leg very badly. We got through to Guildford where the conductor on the rail motor, who was first aid qualified, had a quick look at him and said, 'I wouldn't keep going if I was you – it looks pretty bad.' So we rang up Burnie and they said, 'Well, do you think you and Johnny could do it on your own today? It's a once-off.' I said, 'Oh well, we'll have a go at it.' The only other option would have been to wait for them to round up another fireman and send him up from Burnie. Ray was carted off on a ganger's trolley to meet an ambulance at Hampshire, and John and I took over the job of three men, and we still had nearly the whole day ahead of us.

So I drove and John fired. John was courting a lady at the time, and he remarked to me that he 'hadn't had too late a night' the previous evening. Things went all right and we got down to Primrose. We dropped off the empties and picked up the loaded trucks. Then we took water and coaled up by ourselves – about four tons. We always left Primrose with a full tender of coal. On the return run, John and I fired together up the Que and the Boco hills, both of which were four miles of 1 in 40 grades. I just set the regulator and grabbed the other shovel and John and I took it in turns. This was okay until she started to slip, then I'd quickly drop the shovel and close the regulator. This was in the days of screw couplings, which were much weaker than automatic couplings, so you had to be very careful with your train handling. If you used too much regulator when the couplings were slack, you could easily pull the train apart. Luckily we got away with it.

It was quite late at night by the time we rolled down through Highclere. I noticed that John hadn't put on a fire for the short climb out of Ridgley, so I looked across and said, 'Hey John, you'd better start putting a fire on.' No response. I looked at him again, and he was leaning up against the window, looking like he was completely exhausted. He'd just had it. 'I'm absolutely buggered', he said. We had to wait for a bit at Ridgley to build up steam before we headed off again. It was getting on towards midnight by the time we arrived back at Burnie and knocked off for the night, and I was dog tired, too. 'Never again', I later said to Fred Bartley, the Traffic Superintendent.

Beyer Garratt No. 12 at Farrell Junction in 1961. ~ Frank Kelly, Bernie Kelly collection

16

THE LOG TRUCK

One time in about 1960 we were coming home with an ore train, and I was the senior fireman on a Beyer Garratt. A bloke by the name of Jimmy Norton-Smith was driving, and we were approaching the pulp road crossing at the 22 mile point. It was snowing and was a shocking day for weather. I looked up through the snow, and here were two log trucks coming along towards the crossing. Then one decided to pass the other – it seemed they were having a bit of a race to see who could get up the top of the hill first. I said to Smithy, 'LOOK OUT!' The truck driver didn't see us until he was right on us, and he swung the wheel hard. The truck hit the side of the loco. The impact broke the chains holding the logs and off they went, but remarkably the truck never turned over.

We pulled up and got down to see if he was all right, and all he could say was, 'Me truck, me truck – look what you've done to me truck!' And it did look like a new truck, too. I said, 'I didn't do anything to your truck.' He said, 'Look at the mess you've made of me truck, I was going to put it in the Launceston Show next week. So I said, 'You can still put it in the Launceston Show – as an example of what not to do when there's a train coming. You didn't see us at all, did you?' He replied, 'No, I didn't. You ran into me. I've been driving up here for months, and I've never seen a train on this crossing.' I said, 'Well, there was one here today!'

DRIVER REG FLIGHT

One of the real characters on the EBR was Driver Reg Flight, or 'Gander' as they used to call him. Reg was famous for possessing a very, very short temper. He was an Irishman, and he really displayed his Irishness. While everything was going well he was in a good mood, but when something went wrong – look out!

One day we were bringing a late afternoon train home with one of the Beyers, and we'd reached Guildford and filled up with water. Then we headed over to the refresh for a 'social drink', which although was not in the rule book, was certainly standard practice. The driver always exchanged the staff, then after having a beer put the staff in its clip in the loco cab.

LEFT: On 8 March 1964, ASG 16 at Guildford heads the last steam hauled train to Zeehan, a very popular enthusiast special. The various company houses visible at left of picture were owned by the EBR and the AFH (Australian Forestry Holdings). ~ Michael Schrader, Train Hobby Publications

We left Guildford, and the usual practice was for the driver to hop out of his seat and let one of the firemen take it through to Hampshire. This day it was me. So I sat in the driver's seat, and we were down towards the Wey River when I said to Reg, 'What did you do with that staff?' He said, 'It's there in the clip holder.' I said, 'There's nothing in the clip holder.' Then he said, 'Didn't I give it to you?' I said, 'No, you didn't give it to me, you had it on the bar at Guildford.' 'Well', said Reg, 'I reckon it's still on the bar at Guildford – oh no, what are we going to do? I suppose we'll just have to go without it.' So we got down to the 22½ mile crossing, where a car had pulled up. I said, 'Maybe it's Kevin Burridge, the porter from Guildford.' 'Christ', said Reg, 'I hope so.' Sure enough, here was Kevin at the crossing with his hands up, so we pulled up and he handed us the staff. Dear old Reg thanked him and shook his hand. We got to Hampshire, and the guard came up and said, 'Why'd you stop at the 22 crossing – did you hit that car?' 'No, no', said Reg, 'A bloke pulled us up there, he had a message for us.' The guard must have twigged as to what was going on, as he asked no further questions!

THE PIE AND THE GAUGE GLASS

I was firing for Reg on one occasion on a Beyer Garratt. Reg always used to have a billy of tea on the engine, and he also had a beer bottle full of tea to drink on the way down. His wife used to bake beautiful pasties for him, and he'd put these behind the lubricator on the way down so they would be nice and warm for the return trip. This day he had a pie, and it wasn't quite warm enough, so he put it behind the gauge glass to get hot.

We had left Primrose with a full load, but the engine being cold meant no superheated steam was available. From Primrose we began ascending the short section known as the Bobadil – a very steep grade with deep cuttings which were notorious for always being wet and slippery. All of a sudden, 'BANG', the gauge glass blew, and we had a mad panic to shut the steam off as quickly as we could. We just got over Bobadil when Reg said, 'Oh, we've got a bit of downhill running to the Pieman River, I'll have my pie now.' I burst out laughing – I couldn't help it. He said, 'What are you laughing at?' I said, 'Your pie, or the remains of it, was behind that gauge glass!' Reg was ropeable, and he certainly didn't see the funny side of it.

THE ZEEHAN EXPRESS

At Christmas and New Year we'd often run the ASGs on passenger trains, all the way from Burnie to Zeehan and back in one day. We used to have up to eight carriages, and these days could extend to 16 hours or more. On one occasion we had three derailments on the way back from Zeehan, when one of the trailing driving wheels kept hopping off the track. We had a fettler travelling with us, and by the time we had our third derailment, we knew what we were doing, and we had the wheels back on before the guard even had time to walk to the front of the train. We arrived back at Burnie quite late that night. It turned out that the problem was caused by worn axle box liners.

DRIVING DAYS

I qualified for driving in 1957 at the age of 20, but I had to wait until I turned 21 to drive, as this was the legal age in Tasmania to drive steam locomotives. The chap who passed me for my Government exam said, 'Well, for what it's worth, you have the honour of being the youngest qualified steam driver in Tasmania.' The examination for fireman and driver qualification was the standard Tasmanian Government Railways exam, including steam and diesel. The rules and regulations were virtually the same as on the TGR, although the ERB's track and infrastructure was in better condition than that of the TGR. We often had visitors from the mainland going on cab rides on the EBR, and they always commented on how good the track was.

You had to learn as a driver that there were certain places along the track where you had to power going downhill to drag a loaded train up the other side, and in other sections, a heavy train could push you for miles. I often used to wonder how the guards put up with it – it must have been very rough at times back in the van. All the locos and rolling stock on the EBR were fitted with vacuum brakes, and we never had any great problems with them. There were only two runaway trains during my time on the railway.

THE DIESEL ERA

I loved working on the steam, but it was not to last, as the diesel locos were on their way. The introduction of diesels and the phasing out of steam on the EBR occurred in the early 1960s. The first diesel locomotive obtained by the company was PVH1, an 0-8-0 configuration diesel hydraulic. It was one of the first diesel hydraulic locos to operate in Australia. PVH1 arrived at Burnie on 18 September 1953, and went into traffic shortly afterwards. Whilst the loco reduced running costs considerably, it did have several expensive breakdowns. It was painted a deep green colour at first and became known around the railway as the 'Pride of Erin', although the crews always called it the 'Green Grasshopper'. It was only really a yard shunter, but that didn't stop it from being used out on the main line. The PVH was a terrible thing to ride in, as it didn't have bogies, so it used to kick its way around the curves. The noise going downhill when the throttle was closed, and the transmission was screaming, was really something to hear. The trouble was, you heard it for hours and hours afterwards, too!

The first three of the 10 class diesel hydraulic locos arrived in August 1963, built by Walkers in Queensland and fitted with Paxman engines. Then in 1966, another 10 class was assembled in Launceston, to the same design. When they first came out they just ran with one loco on a train, but then in the late 1960s they started running with two, and then four locos coupled together. The 10 class never had any sort of gangway to walk between them, so you had to step across while you were travelling, and walk around the cabs on these little ledges while clutching the handrails, which was very dangerous. They eventually had walkways fitted. The 10 class were so successful that in 1969, with the increase of traffic on the line, the EBR purchased seven 11 class locomotives from Walkers – five in 1969 and two in 1971 – all fitted with Caterpillar engines. This made a fleet of four 10 class and seven 11 class. Of course with the new locos, new wagons were needed, so the X class wagons were built.

The diesels were very successful and saved the company a lot of money, and before too long, the old steam engines began being cut up for scrap metal. In those days, virtually everything cut up for scrap went to Japan. This was a sad occasion, particularly for a lot of the boiler makers, many of whom had worked on those boilers all their life. When the last of the Beyer Garratts was being cut up, some of us went to have a look – paying our respects, if you like. The manager, Mr. McCormick, was there. Just as they were about to start cutting up the last of them, I turned to him and said, 'What a pity we couldn't keep one of these locos for static display, as they were the first of their type in Australia.' And I well remember him saying, 'Boy, if you've got the money we'll get for the copper tubes and the firebox and so on, you can have the loco.' So that was that. I don't know if there were too many railway preservation societies as such in Tasmania in the mid 1960s.

The introduction of diesels caused quite a change to our lives – particularly as the fireman had nothing to do – but we all just got used to them after a while.

PVH1 diesel hydraulic loco, renumbered 21, ready to depart Primrose in April 1962.
~ Keith Atkinson, Train Hobby Publications

THE GANGER'S TROLLEY

One tragic accident occurred during my long career on the EBR, in the diesel days. I was driving a train of empties between Ridgley and Highclere, heading for Primrose, and around a blind corner came a Casey trolley, with about eight blokes on board. This was a hell of a shock. I put the brake handle into emergency, but both train and trolley were doing about 25 mph, so we collided, and the trolley was smashed to pieces – there were bits of trolley all over the place. Most of the blokes jumped off, and a couple of them leapt right over the fence and landed in the adjacent pig yard. Another fettler landed in a thick clump of blackberries, and although he was uninjured, it took about half an hour to extract him. An ambulance came up from Burnie and carted the injured fettlers off to hospital, and eventually we were cleared to resume our run.

When we got back to Burnie later that day, the EBR's head mechanic came and took out the speed recorder rolls for examination. We went up to front the manager, Mr. Fagan, and his first question wasn't, 'How are you?', or 'What sort of a day have you had?', but was simply 'What speed were you doing?' I said, 'Approximately 25 mph, why?' Then he said abruptly, 'I'll ask the questions, thank you. Are you sure you were doing 25 mph?' I said, 'Look, the mechanic has just taken the speedometer rolls out, it will be on the chart.' 'But', he said, 'don't you know exactly what speed you were doing?' I replied, 'Do you think I'm going to be looking at the speedo with a ganger's trolley coming towards us?' He was a good man, Mr. Fagan, but this was not one of his better performances, and it was quite obvious to me that management were convinced, for some reason, that we were exceeding the speed limit.

The next day we found out that one of the fettlers – my uncle – had died of his injuries, which was shocking news, although when we collided I'd expected there to be far more injuries and fatalities than there were. Trolleys didn't travel on the staff – they just made a telephone call and received clearance, but this morning the ganger insisted the train had been and gone. A couple of the fettlers disputed this, but the ganger insisted, and basically told them to get on the trolley or they wouldn't have a day's work. The train was in fact about half an hour late this particular morning, due to the guard having slept in, and a replacement guard having to be located.

At the subsequent inquiry, the train crew were cleared of any wrongdoing, as the ganger had proceeded into the section without obtaining clearance. The ganger was demoted to the position of fettler. Had we been over the speed limit, I subsequently discovered, we could have been had up on a manslaughter charge, even though the gang had no right to be in the section. This really brought home to me the importance of never exceeding the speed limit.

ABOVE: Tasmanian Government Railways locomotive V9 at Rosebery in October 1962. This loco was used only between Rosebery and Zeehan, and hauled the last goods train from Zeehan in 1965. ~ Bernie Kelly

RIGHT: For a period in the 1980s, the EBR ran long trains hauled by multiple locomotives. In November 1987, nine diesel locos ease a heavy concentrates train down the 1 in 33 grades into Burnie. ~ Peter Ralph

In October 1997, the centenary train crosses the Bastyan Dam over 'new' Pieman bridge. ~ Peter Ralph

BECOMING A TRAFFIC CONTROLLER

For about twelve months in the mid 1990s there were no copper concentrates coming through from Queenstown, which meant a major restructure for the EBR. About 23 people ended up off the payroll and had to find work elsewhere during this period. I was transferred to the traffic section and initially worked loading trains, so I virtually became a porter! By this time, many of the smaller items were going through to the west coast by private road contractor, but the heavy mining equipment and timber and so on all still went by rail. I spent three or four years doing this job before moving into the Traffic Office as a Trainee Traffic Controller.

When a train arrived at a staff station, the guard would ring the station ahead to check whether there were any fettlers on the track before proceeding into the section. Of course the station masters would be in contact with Burnie Train Control to see where the trains were, and the line had a timetable to work to. Total radio coverage had been achieved throughout the system by this time.

As a Traffic Controller, things could get pretty busy. You were in communication with the trains and the gangs, and by radio with the shunters working in Burnie yard. We were also effectively the railway switchboard after five o'clock, and you had the general public ringing up about various things. You'd take messages for blokes. We used to do a lot of paperwork. We handled the sulphuric acid deliveries. You'd have trucks coming in to pick up loading to be taken to various places around the state. You'd organise the rosters for the train crews. Sometimes you had to make decisions on behalf of the boss after he'd gone home, or if he was away. So for all intents and purposes, I was in charge of the railway.

The EBR centenary in 1997 was a tremendous occasion, and saw the return of steam to the line. Then in 1998 the line was taken over by an American concern called Wisconsin Central, and was later integrated into Tasrail. I was the last of the original Emu Bay employees to remain when all of this took place, and it was a pretty hard time, with no one sure who was going to be employed and who wasn't. On Monday 31 August 1998, I took retirement, after almost 44 years with the company.

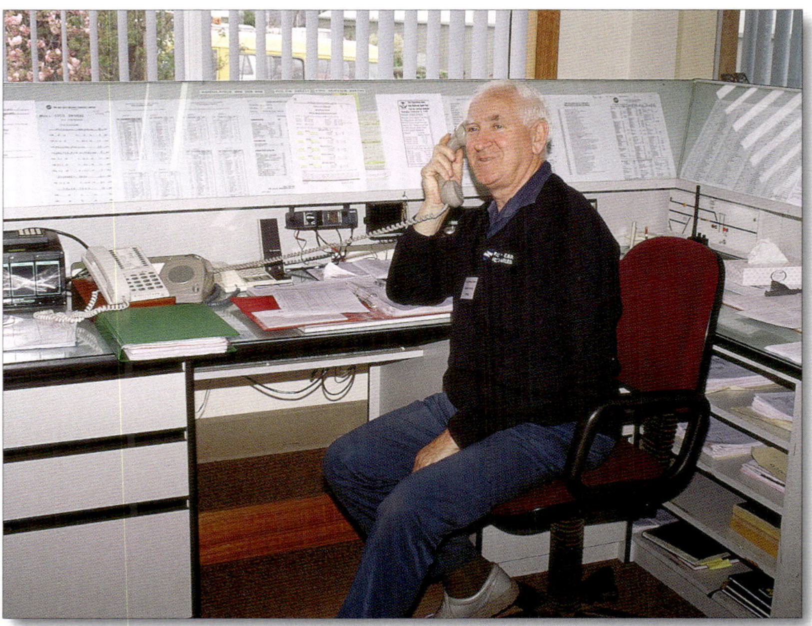

UPPER RIGHT: The 1997 Emu Bay Railway centenary celebrations tour. Led by the newly restored Dübs loco No. 8, the train is seen passing through Moory Junction en route to Rosebery in October 1997.

LOWER RIGHT: Traffic Controller Hedley Charles at work at the Burnie office. October 1997. ~ Both images Peter Ralph

Travels in Western Tasmania

PETER RALPH

JANUARY 1953

My desire to visit the rugged West Coast of Tasmania came as a teenager, after reading Geoffrey Blainey's famous book, *The Peaks of Lyell*. This fine book described the mining and railway operations of the area, and certainly aroused my curiosity.

In January 1953, a mate and I went on a six week cycling tour of the Apple Isle, and after riding from Hobart across to the West Coast, I had my first glimpse of the famous mining settlement of Queenstown – and what an impression it was! I could never forget the rugged nature of the terrain, the denuded hills and the gravel football ground.

To get from Queenstown up to Burnie on the North Coast, we travelled by trains over three different systems – the Mount Lyell Railway to Strahan, then the Tasmanian Government Railway train to Zeehan, where the connection would be made with the Emu Bay Railway. We slept rough on Queenstown's station platform to ensure we wouldn't miss the early departure, and after putting our bikes in the guards van, we travelled on the morning passenger train over the famous Abt rack railway to Strahan, and marvelled at the spectacular scenery en route.

We then travelled on the government line from Strahan to Zeehan, where we had a short wait before the departure of EBR's Gardner rail motor, WG1. This was in the days before the road went through to the West Coast, so the railway was all there was. The service was still used by locals living along the line, and we were certainly the only tourists on board. The motor stopped at all the stations such as Primrose and Farrell, and people used the train to go shopping in Burnie, etc. It just ambled along without any hurry, and a smattering of passengers got on and off. I was enthralled by the scenery along the way which was wonderful, with large sections of thick rainforest and drizzly rain, so typical of Tasmania's West Coast. We stopped at Guildford for half an hour and made good use of the wonderful tea room there. It was run by a lovely lady who sold cups of tea, along with fresh pies and scones. The trip to Burnie took just over four hours, and we arrived late in the afternoon.

LEFT: In November 1957, ASG No. 16 hauls a goods train across the Pieman River bridge. ~ Peter Ralph

NOVEMBER 1957

In 1957 I again visited Burnie and travelled right through to Zeehan by goods train. Travelling in the guard's van was permitted, which made for a very interesting experience. The guard and engine crews were friendly and accommodating, and on the return trip I managed to secure a ride in the loco cab. The crew could see that I was a keen photographer, so on the approach to the Pieman Bridge they stopped to let me off for a photograph. The only problem was that they couldn't stop and pick me up on the other side of the bridge, as they had a 1 in 40 grade to contend with and would have had difficulty lifting the 250 ton load from a standing start. No problem, I thought. I sprinted across the bridge and took up my vantage point, and the train stormed over the bridge. The train picked up speed rapidly, and as I leapt aboard the guard's van it felt as if my arms would be ripped out of their sockets! This section of track was later bypassed, and the old bridge lies submerged under the dark and brooding waters of the Bastyan Dam.

Walker Gardner rail motor at Farrell Junction in 1957. ~ Peter Ralph

EBR ENGINEMAN 1942-1986

GEOFF BROWN

Career engineman Geoff Brown spent 44 years on the Emu Bay Railway, from 1942 to 1986. In March 2013 he recalled some of his enduring memories of the job.

JOINING THE EBR

I grew up in the west coast mining town of Waratah, and joined the Emu Bay Railway in January 1942, just before turning 18. I started work at Burnie, and at first I was a real dogs-body – I did a bit of everything, but mostly labouring. Then I became an engine cleaner. In 1943 I had a stint as engine cleaner at Zeehan, in the days when the EBR carted ore from Rosebery to Zeehan for smelting. This was mainly zinc from the EZ mine. After it was cooked at Zeehan, we'd drag it back to Burnie and it would be railed to the zinc works at Hobart for processing. I also remember from this time exploring the engine shed of the old North East Dundas Tramway, which had closed a few years earlier. One of the K class Garratts was still inside, along with all sorts of bits and pieces of engines scattered around.

It was a long apprenticeship – six years in my case – to become a fully qualified fireman. I spent many a long shift firing the Beyer Garratts, the ASGs, and also on the Dübs, along with the shunting engines at Burnie.

Plenty of memorable things happened. Once I was firing for Cyril Butt, and as we were going along near Hampshire he suddenly called out, 'Look out boy, we're gonna hit a cow.' We hit the cow all right – 'PLOMP'. I stuck my head out of the cab to have a look and I said, 'You better pull up Cyril, it's stuck between the bogies on the tender.' But he was having none of it. He said, 'No, no, no. If I pull up, what are you going to do with it? If ever you get 'em like that', he said, 'you just keep going and it'll eventually get crunched up before we're finished.' He was right – after a while it got mangled up under the wheels and was finally spat out the back of the train. There was nothing much else you could do.

Derelict Krauss locomotives from the old Zeehan tramways pictured at Zeehan in December 1956. ~ Ray Bruce, Neil Tate collection

ZEEHAN

By now it was 1948, and I was sent to Zeehan as a fully qualified fireman, where I was to stay for two years. From Zeehan, we normally only ran as far as Boco siding and back again, although when things went wrong, we could find ourselves much closer to Burnie. I spent many days running the mail train with a Dübs loco. We used to stop at Renison Bell, Rosebery, Primrose and Farrell siding, and some of the old fellows used to grizzle about us arriving late at Boco – they reckoned we used to lose time on purpose!

I boarded at the Zeehan pub back then, and the sandwiches they'd give you were so boring. You'd have roast lamb today, and roast beef tomorrow, then roast lamb the next day – you'd get sick of the sight of them. Now the Guildford refreshment rooms were

A rare colour photograph of Zeehan's rambling railway yard and sheds, pictured in December 1956. In the foreground, loaded coal wagons and an empty G wagon occupy sidings either side of the main line. In the background at left is the tiny Tasmanian Government Railways office, next to the coal stage and water tank – a tank renowned for its poor quality water. The TGR owned all three of the engine sheds pictured. The shed at left, with a Beyer Garratt locomotive visible, also housed the resident TGR loco. The forlorn remains of the 2 ft gauge Hagans engine can be seen in front of the sheds. ~ Ray Bruce, Neil Tate collection

supposed to have the best sandwiches in Australia – everything was made fresh – so I used to ring up Guildford from Boco and get them to send me down a few bob's worth of sandwiches and other stuff on the rail motor.

Sometimes we'd cook up a feed on the footplate. I remember one time a well-dressed man came up at Boco and spoke to us. I was busily cooking a feed on the firing shovel – steak, sausages and eggs. I told him to climb up, and up he came. He introduced himself, and he was some big wig in the chemical business from England. He said, 'I've been fortunate enough to travel all around the world on railways, but I've never smelt anything as good as that.' I said, 'Would you like a piece of steak?' 'No thanks', he said, 'the guard's already put an order in at Guildford, but oh God that smells good.'

UP

Mileage			No. 2 GOODS Mon. to Fri. inc.	No. 4 PASSENGER Mon. to Sat. inc.	No. 6 ORE Mon. to Sat. inc.	No. 8 ORE Monday Con.	No. 10 ORE As required Con.
			a.m.	a.m.	p.m.	p.m.	p.m.
—	ZEEHAN	D	8.45				
9	REN. BELL	D	9.15				
17	ROSEBERY	A	9.45				
		D	10.30	11.50			
18	PRIMROSE	A	10.35 x 1, 3, 5				
		D	11.15		12.8	3.5	10.40
24	FARRELL	A					
		D	11.50	p.m. 12.14	12.40	3.30	11.10
30	BOKO	A	p.m. 12.25 passed by 4 x 7 Monday				
		D	12.47	12.32 Pass 2 x 7 Monday	x 7 Mon. 1.10	4.0	11.40
50	GUILDFORD (R)	A	2.17	1.37	2.45	5.35	
		D	2.45	1.47	3.0	5.50 x 9	a.m. 1.15
68	HAMPSHIRE	D	3.45	2.33	4.0	7.10	2.15
88	BURNIE	A	4.55	3.30	5.10	8.20	3.25

Road Motor to and from Waratah connects at Guildford with Burnie-Rosebery Motor in mornings only.
Passenger Trains connect with road bus at Rosebery for Renison Bell, Zeehan and Queenstown.
(R) — Refreshments.
B. P. FAGAN, Manager

Geoff Brown carried this battered EBR Working Timetable while firing at Zeehan in 1948. Note pencilled comment next to mileage column! ~ Geoff Brown collection

*On this timetable, 'Boco' – named for Boco Creek – is referred to as 'Boko'. Through the years, the EBR seemed unable to decide which spelling to use. 'Boco' appears in most references, but on some timetables and documents, and even on the station building itself, the name was often spelt 'Boko'.

Enginemen Daryl Luke (left) and Geoff Brown in front of diesel loco 1003 in the 1960s. ~ Daryl Luke collection

DRIVING DAYS

I went back to Burnie in 1950 and soon qualified as a driver. The biggest challenge for any driver was running trains up and down the steep sections of the track, particularly the Que Hill, between Guildford and Bulgobac. This section had a series of sharp curves on a 1 in 40 gradient, and was notorious for wet, greasy rails. Sometimes in winter the snow could be a problem, although I used to like driving in the snow to a certain extent. On the old steam locos, the snow tended to deaden the sounds of all the rattles. A couple of times it was so deep the loco just couldn't cope, and it covered the ends of the sand pipes, so you couldn't get sand under the wheels. On these occasions we'd leave our loaded wagons at the bottom of the Que and we'd run up with just the loco, dropping sand up and back. Then we'd pick up the load and have another go. In all my years on the job, we never once left a train up there. It was often a battle, but we always made it through somehow.

Not all the rolling stock was well braked in earlier times, either. Once when I was a young fireman we were heading off down the Que with a load of the old ballast wagons, which were very heavy, and only had basic brakes. As we started down the hill, my mate, Hilton Sharpe, called out to me, 'Hang on, we're not going to stop this lot.' So we tore down the hill, around all the curves, and it wasn't until we reached the bottom that she started to slow down. As the tender bumped along I managed to get a couple of extra turns out of the handbrake, but that didn't make much difference. Sharpy must have got onto them about this afterwards, because soon enough they brought out a rule which required 50% brakes on a train, or we weren't to go. Some of the ore trucks never had vacuum brakes at all in those days. When we took ore from Rosebery to Zeehan to get cooked up, many of the trucks we were using were TGR wagons and many didn't have vacuum brake pans at all. We had some pretty hairy downhill runs at times with these trains!

We had a lot of trouble lifting the loaded ore trains up the 1 in 40 grade at Farrell, but we had a good trick to overcome this. After we'd stopped at Farrell, we'd back up, with the guard keeping a lookout, and lay sand all the way down as we went. Then when we got to a straight section we'd open her up and give it to her, and we always managed to lift the load this way. There was one old driver who spent nearly an hour trying to get out of Farrell siding with a Beyer, and eventually he did his nut and took two Z wagons off and shoved them in the siding. A full load for a Beyer was seven Z wagons, and the two he took off comprised the profit for the train, so the manager got onto him and told him that if he ever did that again, he'd be sacked on the spot.

We used to cart a heap of logs to the sawmill at Bulgobac, where timber was sawn for use at the Rosebery mine. We'd load these logs anywhere along the track – you'd just pull up wherever they were being cut. The Bulgobac sawmill had a two foot gauge horse tramway operating for years, right up to the 1960s. The tram crossed the EBR line, and horses came up twice a day or so, with two or three logs trailing behind them to be taken up into the mill. The rule book stated that the tram had to wait for the train, but I figured rules were there to be broken. They'd always pull their horses up to wait, but they were big draft horses and they were straining with an uphill load, so I'd pull the train up and wave them through! I doubt if anyone ever knew I did this – and I was certainly never asked about it.

THE KOMBI VAN

We used to carry motor vehicles on the train between Rosebery and Guildford and vice versa, and one day we had a bloke put his Volkswagen Kombi Van on the train. This day we derailed twice on the Burnie side of the Pieman River, and this fellow became quite upset. The second time we came off the road, I could hear him grizzling before I even got to the derailed wagon. He bailed me up and started going crook at me, ranting and raving. I said, 'Don't blame me, it's not my bloody railway. 'Well, you're the driver. What's wrong with the bloody railways, anyway? I might never get my bus to Guildford the way we're going', he said. I couldn't resist having a dig at him. I said, 'You could be right mate. I'll give you £5 for it.' Well, he barked and he roared – he made more noise than a Tasmanian Tiger! We found out afterwards that the derailments were due to a tyre on one of the old wagons being an inch shorter than normal, which explained why it was dropping off on the tight curves. It should never have been allowed out on the mainline in the first place.

WHERE'S THE TRAIN?

One time in 1950 we were at Farrell doing a shunt with a Dübs. After a while I said to my mate, 'Gee, the bloody guard's taking his time, I wonder what he's doing?' So I went back to have a look, just as the guard came trudging around the corner. He was red in the face, and in a panic. He said 'It's gone!' I said, 'What's gone?' 'The train', he said. Farrell was on a steep hill, and when we'd split the train to do the shunt, the last two trucks had run away. I said, 'Didn't you put the handbrake on?' 'No', he replied, 'I thought the vacuum brakes would hold.' When he realised the trucks had rolled away he went tearing off after them, but he never

A Beyer Garratt loco pounds up the hill between Burnie and Ridgley with the morning train. November 1962. ~ Bernie Kelly

had a hope in the world of catching them. So I sat my fireman up on the tender to keep a good lookout and we went down cautiously with the loco. It was about three miles down to the Pieman bridge, and when we got there we pulled up and had a look down in the river, but we saw nothing. I thought, where the bloody hell could the trucks be? Then we saw them, derailed way up the hill towards Rosebery, and the track was a mess. One of the trucks was full of mine tailings, which were heavy, so they must have really been hammering by the time they reached the bridge, and they'd derailed just beyond it. The track was completely buggered – it was all out of gauge, and there were bits of smashed sleepers and fish plates and bolts – you name it. I said, 'Well, that's buggered that, we can't get the loco anywhere near it.' So we went to Boco looking for the gang. The ganger, Harold Jones, told us we were lucky. The previous day, the permanent way inspector had been following this train in his little Morris van, and if the trucks had rolled back and crunched him, he would have been killed for sure. The guard was in all sorts of trouble when the boss turned up at Boco. I was standing outside the office, and I could hear a lot of yelling going on inside! The guard got off the hook though, because a week later the Beyer turned over down at the Brooklyn Road crossing near Burnie, and this took the heat off him.

NO DRAWBARS

On Mondays, two Beyer Garratts would be sent down to Primrose to pick up the weekend stuff, a total of fourteen loaded Z wagons. There was never double heading in the steam days, as two locos would have ripped the couplings apart – we pulled enough couplings apart as it was! So the trains were short but very heavy, until years later when they began running multi-unit trains with the diesels. We always carried spare couplings and drawbars in the van. On one occasion I was heading home with Daryl Luke. We left Guildford and when we reached the first little dip in the track, one of the drawbars ripped apart. We fixed that, but no sooner had we got going again than we did another one. Each time we had to go back to the van and get spare parts, and it took us about an hour and a half to get two miles out of Guildford. The guard said to me, 'You better be careful with this lot – we're running out of couplings and drawbars!'

THE FROGS AND THE WATER TANK

One old driver, Ray Claridge, ran out of water on an ASG coming up out of Ring Hill one day. They waited there for hours and hours, and finally a TGR loco had to be brought out from Zeehan to tow them in. This made the train terribly late. It turned out they'd stopped at Rosebery, and after cleaning the fire they turned on the hose to flush out the ash pan. Unfortunately, they forgot to turn the hose off afterwards, so as they were running around shunting Rosebery yard for a fair while, all their water from the tank was running out all over the ground from this three inch pipe. After they'd finished shunting, they went to water the loco, but the tank was bone dry! So they had to keep going and hope they'd make it through to Zeehan, but they didn't! The boss confronted Ray and asked him what happened. 'Old Unc', as they used to call him, said to the boss, 'The frogs must have drank all the water.'

WEE GEORGIE WOOD

At Farrell we used to pull up alongside *Wee Georgie Wood*, and seeing this little engine next to a Beyer was quite a sight! The driver did it all on this little railway – driver, guard, ticket seller – the lot. The Tullah mob used to buy coal through the EBR, and we'd take a couple of wagons up when we had a shipment, but sometimes they'd run out. When this happened, we'd pull up right alongside and shovel a bit of coal straight onto *Wee Georgie*, and nobody ever found out. We'd pick out a bit of Maitland coal, and about eight or ten good shovels full and you'd fill him up.

One time I landed at Farrell with a Beyer, and here was *Georgie* lying on his side with smoke and steam oozing out of him. I called out to one of the blokes, 'How'd you come to put *Georgie* there?' The fellow said, 'We thought we'd copy you and do a bit of 'fly' shunting with that coal wagon, but we got tangled up with the points, split them, and ended up like this.' The blokes weren't at all concerned – they reckoned they could get him back on without too much trouble. Another time I came into Farrell and here was *Georgie* in the turntable pit, smoking and steaming – they'd forgotten to set the road and just drove him straight in!

ABOVE: Workmen discharging gravel at a construction project site near Renison Bell. The inspection car pictured is the company's 1938 Chevrolet. 4 January 1957.

RIGHT: Farrell Junction, also known as Farrell Siding, presents a busy scene as an ASG loco shunts the yard. In the background, North Mount Farrell Krauss locomotive No. 9 can be seen charging uphill towards the junction, in an impressive display of steam and smoke. 4 January 1957.
~ Both images Ray Bruce, Neil Tate collection

A 473

Diesels and lupins at Guildford. ~ John Watkins, Burnie Regional Museum

THE DIESELS

We grizzled a bit when the diesels came out, as there wasn't much to do, whereas on the steam locos you'd just put your head down and your behind up and go. But we got used to them after a while. We were threatened with all sorts of things if we were caught sleeping on the diesel locos, but they would tend to put you to sleep, with their rhythm and vibration. After the *Southern Aurora* smash in Victoria in 1969, vigilance control buttons were fitted to all the locos. This was enforced by the insurance company, who basically demanded it.

Some of the drivers took a while to get used to the diesels, though. At that time the Z wagons only had one vacuum pan on them, and when you came down from the EZ yard at Primrose, the trains had trouble stopping. To assist braking, the old steam drivers used to wind the engines into reverse gear and open the regulator a bit. So when the PVH diesel first came out, one of the drivers tried this trick with it, but when he put it in reverse it blew up – he'd done it so many times with a steam loco, it just came naturally. They reckoned the damage bill for the PVH was about £10,000, so eventually all the Z wagons were fitted with an extra vacuum pan.

The diesels could scoop holes in the rails if they slipped badly enough. One time a drum of oil came loose from a train going down the Que hill, which was on a 1 in 40 grade. It dropped down in between two wagons and got crushed, with oil going all over the rails. Of course when the next train came up the hill it slipped and slid all the way up, scooping holes in the tracks as it went, and they were so bad the gang had to re-rail the whole section. When the wheels on a diesel spun badly at night, they looked like 'Catherine Wheels', with a shower of sparks going in all directions. One time a ganger gave one of the new fettlers a drum of grease, and told him to grease the curves up the Que hill. So off he went, and he greased the curves all right – including the tops of the rails and all! He didn't know any better, poor fellow. Of course you can imagine the trouble the next train to come through had!

There were many places along the track where you just knew you were going to slip, so you'd start putting sand down in advance and you never had any trouble after that. Then, in its wisdom, the company fitted automatic sanding equipment to all the diesel locos, and one time I had a barney with the manager about them. 'You've got the cheek to tell me that after we spent all that money on those automatic sanders, you think you can do a better job than them', he said to me. 'Yes', I replied. 'Oh, come off it', he growled. The boss wouldn't listen to me, he just reckoned I was cranky. But then most of the bosses were like that – they always reckoned they knew everything. But it was true – if you thought you were about to slip, you pressed your manual sand button, but if you left it until you started slipping and the automatic sand applied, it caused the throttle to back off, and you'd slow right down. At one time they even brought out an official regulation which said not to put sand under a slipping wheel, but these automatic sanders only worked when the wheels were slipping, so it contradicted the regulations – they were just asking for trouble.

One time in the diesel days, I was with Daryl Luke on the Que. At one point, a heap of trees had slid down the embankment and were blocking the line, so we pulled her up. They were big lumps of trees, too, and they would have smashed the cab to pieces had we run into them. We managed to get onto Burnie, and the boss, the Traffic Superintendent, said, 'You've got an axe in your toolbox, haven't you?' I said, 'Look, I wouldn't give that axe to my wife to cut sticks for my heater.' He said, 'Why is that?' I said, 'When we first got here I had a go at one tree with the axe, and it never even left a mark on it! 'Well, what do you intend to do?', said the TS. I replied, 'Well, you better organise the fettlers to come down with some chainsaws.' 'Aargh', he said, 'it will take too long. I said 'We'll still be here at tea time if you don't send them down – they're big lumps of trees.' Anyhow, the fettlers arrived on the scene, and they said, 'Did that silly-looking so and so tell you to cut them with an axe?' We helped them by pulling the trunks out of the way with the loco, but we were still there for a good few hours. The TS said to us later, 'I can't understand how those trees blocked the track – we cleared the track a full 50 feet either side. I said, 'Well, they were about 100 foot tall, that's why.' But I couldn't get through to him – he had something in his mind, and that was that.

Another time we spent about three hours cutting up trees near the Ring River bridge, this time with a sharp axe. When we cut them, they slipped straight down the embankment and into the river. We took it in turns, but after that effort I never wanted to see an axe ever again.

THE PRIMROSE LOADING FACILITY

The ore we carted on the EBR was crushed to a powder, and was taken to the Burnie wharf where an overhead crane grabbed it and tipped it into a big loading bin. At about the same time as the diesel locos were introduced, a tippler was built at Burnie wharf which tipped the whole wagon upside down and emptied it much more quickly. They also built an overhead loading facility at Primrose during this period, and I was one of the first drivers to take a train into it.

Things didn't always go too smoothly at first though, and this day the loader, which went backwards and forwards filling up the trucks, went too far. I could see it coming towards us and I called out to my mate, 'Look out, look out, it's heading straight for us!' The loader went straight past the end of the wagon, passed over the top of us, and dumped a great heap of ore all over the loco! The stuff went everywhere, and there must have been tons of it. It went all over the cab and the running boards, and on the cab steps – you could hardly see out of the windows. The boss nearly had a heart attack when he came down and saw the mess! He apologised profusely to me, but I said, 'Well, if any of it went down the exhaust pipe, it would probably have just been blown straight back out again.' I had a look, but it looked okay. Next thing you knew, all these blokes with shovels turned up, and they spent ages cleaning up the mess. I don't know what happened to the man responsible for loading!

RIGHT: Multi-unit consist near Pieman River in May 1983.
~ Richard Kepert, Train Hobby Publications

THE WEST COASTER

Dübs No. 6 *Murchison*, at Burnie on the *West Coaster* train. ~ Michael Schrader, Train Hobby Publications

As road transport and private car ownership increased during the 1950s, tourism to the West Coast rapidly increased, but with no road connection in existence between Zeehan and Guildford, more and more vehicles were being carried on EBR trains. In 1960 the Zeehan to Rosebery road was completed, leaving a gap of 33 miles between Rosebery and Guildford.

In 1960, following an approach by the Pioneer tour company, and to cater for the increasing vehicle traffic on offer, the EBR introduced a service called the *West Coaster*. Two of the Dübs 4-8-0 locos – No.6 and No.8 – were converted to oil burning and dressed up for the new service, fitted out with smoke deflectors and painted in an attractive two-tone blue. They were named *Murchison* and *Heemskirk* respectively, after two well known local mountains. Several carriages were also refurbished and repainted in the attractive new colour scheme.

The *West Coaster* departed Burnie at 8 o'clock in the morning, and upon arrival at Guildford, the Pioneer Clipper tour coaches and cars were driven up a loading ramp onto flat trucks, where they were lashed down. Passengers then boarded the refurbished carriages, and the train completed its scenic journey through to Rosebery. Here, the cars and coaches were unloaded and the tourists resumed their West Coast road trip. North-bound traffic was then loaded and the engine was reconditioned, before the train returned to Guildford where unloading again occurred. The train arrived back at Burnie by mid afternoon.

The *West Coaster* proved to be an extremely popular and successful venture in its short life, with thousands of vehicles and passengers being carried. The Murchison Highway was put through between Guildford and Rosebery, and by December 1963, demand rapidly fell away, with the service being cancelled in January 1964.

The attractive two-tone blue paint scheme lived on however, as all EBR diesel locomotives received a similar blue livery.

RIGHT: Dübs No. 8 *Heemskirk*, on a Burnie-bound *West Coaster* at Guildford in November 1962. The load of logs in the siding are bound for R.G. Howard's mill at Zeehan. ~ Bernie Kelly

HEEMSKIRK
8

Pioneer Tours

ABOVE: A *West Coaster* train crosses the Pieman River in November 1962.

LEFT: *Heemskirk* drifts downhill from Primrose towards the Pieman River with the *West Coaster*, in November 1962. ~ Both images Bernie Kelly

BELOW: The Murchison Highway opened in late 1963, meaning towns such as Rosebery and Tullah were finally connected to the outside world by road. Before long, trucks were lumbering up and down the West Coast, spelling doom for many of the region's railways and tramways. ~ Peter Ralph

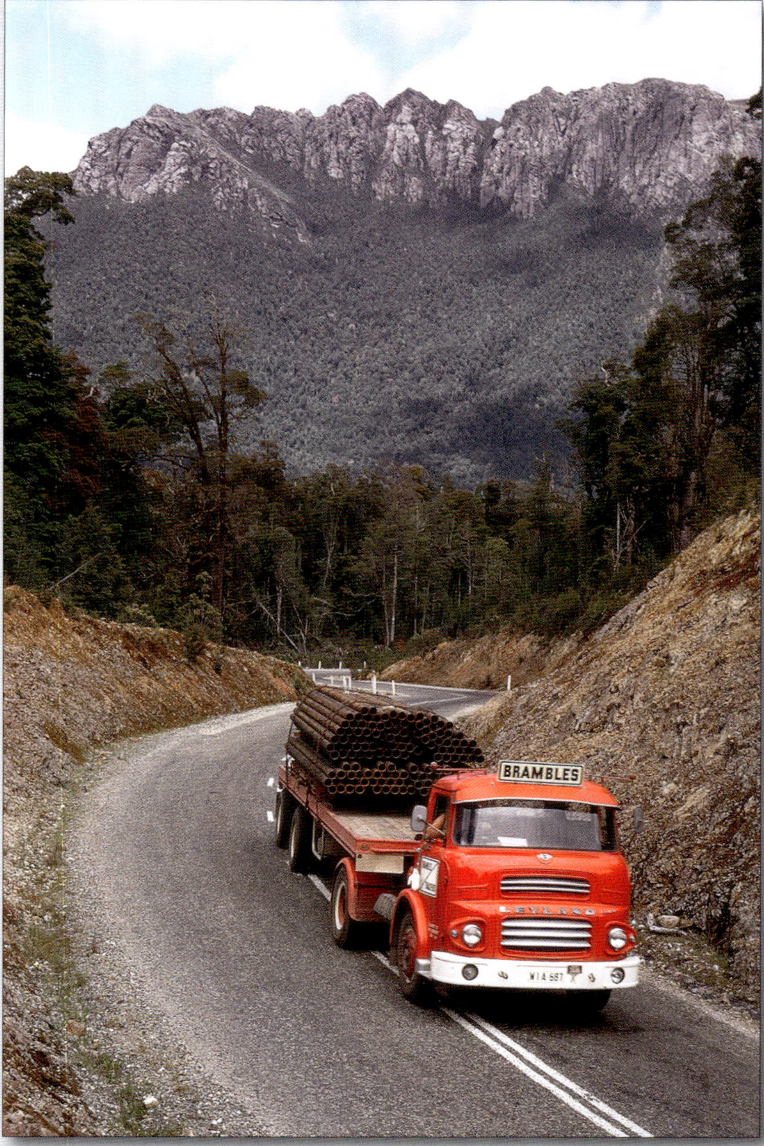

EBR Engineman 1948-1992

DARYL LUKE

At the 1½ mile point, just beyond the Brooklyn Road crossing, a Dübs loco hauls 'The Mail' train towards Zeehan. c.1940.
~ Burnie Regional Museum

Another proud EBR engineman, Daryl Luke operated trains over the West Coast line from 1948 until 1992 – a 44-year career full of memories.

IN THE EARLY DAYS

I was born in the mining town of Waratah in 1929. I was only young, but I remember the two footer Magnet tram, which ran out to the silver lead mine. We called the little engines the 'Coffee Pots', and they had gigantic funnels, which contained spark arrestors. The engines were run mainly on wood, so they were prone to start bushfires.

I joined the EBR in 1948, and by the time I finished in 1992, I was the longest serving employee of the company. It was a long career all right. I began at the age of 19 as a fettler, stationed at Guildford. There were gangs everywhere back then – one each at Burnie, Ridgley, Highclere, two at Guildford, then others at Bulgobac, Rosebery and Zeehan. There were about eight blokes in each gang, and we got around on motorised trolleys, the two stroke Caseys – which we called 'Water Boilers'. Life was all right. The work was fully manual labour, replacing sleepers and manually drilling the dog holes. Our section was from Guildford south through Hatfield to the 49 mile point, at the top of Que Hill, just below McCarty's cutting. The gang from Bulgobac came up to the 49 from the south end. My old man worked with the Rosebery gang, and he used to ride the trike from Bulgobac to Farrell every day.

We worked in the snow now and then, which could get interesting. The snow was knee deep on occasions, and when it was too deep for the Casey trolley, they'd let one of the Beyer Garratts go through with its cowcatcher on the front, and that would clear it away. In about 1950 a train got stuck in the snow at the 45 mile point near Hatfield. They couldn't get going, and they eventually ran out of everything – steam, water and coal.

ENGINE CLEANING

I worked as a fettler for roughly two years, until I went to Burnie in 1950 to become an engine cleaner. Before long, I was sent down to Zeehan. There was just the one crew at Zeehan, one driver, one fireman, one guard and one cleaner, and that was it. The driver at Zeehan had to be his own fitter, too, and he carried a heap of gear to fix whatever might go wrong with the loco. I boarded at the pub, and my job was to get up at 3 o'clock each morning and go to the engine shed for light up. Back then there was no lighting in the town after midnight, so it was absolutely pitch black at that hour, and I never had a torch. I'd make my way down through the tussocks, and one morning I nearly trod on a sleeping cow! We operated out of the old Government shed at Zeehan, as the EBR one, which was way out in the sticks, had burnt down and had never been replaced.

The Station Master at Zeehan was a government man, and was responsible for the TGR line to Strahan. The government line had just a single CCS loco, but on Strahan picnic days they'd bring an extra CCS through from Burnie and put on a double header train from Zeehan to Strahan for the picnics. An EBR crew would have to travel as pilot, although the loco was crewed by TGR men. After my time at Zeehan, I went back to Burnie and began firing on road jobs.

BURNIE IN THE 1950s

The work for engine crews in this period was mostly in daylight hours, and it wasn't until later years, in the diesel era, that they started the night run to Primrose. But it was nothing to work 12 or 14 hours per day in these times. As a result, Burnie crews worked day on, day off. One week you'd work Monday, Wednesday and Friday, then the following week you'd work Tuesday, Thursday and Saturday. There were normally about four trains per day out of Burnie in this era, and there were three cleaners on every shift. The nightshift driver started at 11 pm to prepare the Garratt for the next morning's run, as Garratt locos were always rostered on the ore trains. Then the early crew would come in at 4.00 am to get the Dübs engine ready for 'The Mail', as we always called it. The other engine crews signed on half an hour before their train's departure.

On most days, there was a 6.00 am ore train to Primrose, usually hauled by a Beyer Garratt, then at 6.30 am The Mail departed for Zeehan with a Dübs, followed at 7.35 am by the Zeehan-bound rail motor. On some days, an extra Primrose ore train, known as 'The Calcine', departed at 8 am, usually with an ASG on the front.

After the 6 o'clock ore train left Burnie, the early crew took the Dübs engine down to the station and hooked onto the mixed train, which would have already been marshalled. This crew then did shunting until 12 o'clock. There were two shifts shunting in the yard every day, as the EBR crews did all the shunting for the government trains as well as the EBR trains. Burnie yard was controlled by the EBR – the TGR crews just came in and hopped on their trains and took off.

THE EMU BAY RAILWAY COMPANY LTD.

PASSENGER'S LUGGAGE

BURNIE

ABOVE: EBR luggage label. ~ Don River Railway

LEFT: Burnie yard is a hive of activity on this summer's day in December 1956. ~ Ray Bruce, Neil Tate collection

THE EMU BAY RAILWAY COMPANY LIMITED

Working Time Table (SUNDAY EXCEPTED) To Operate from Monday, March 4, 1957

DOWN

		No. 2 ORE Monday to Saturday inc.	No. 4 GOODS Monday to Friday inc.	No. 6 PASSENGER Monday to Saturday inc.	No. 8 ORE Monday - Conditional
		a.m.	a.m.	a.m.	a.m.
BURNIE	D	5.45	6.15	7.50	8.5
RIDGLEY	D	—	7.12	8.22	
HAMPSHIRE	D	(7.5)	(7.50)	8.50	(9.25)
GUILDFORD	A	8.15	8.50	9.35	
	D	(8.30)	9.10	9.45	(10.45)
BOKO	A		10.25 x 3		12 noon x 1-5
	D	(9.45) x 3	10.53 Passed by 6	10.38 x 3 Pass 4	12.55 p.m.
FARRELL	A				
	D	(10.5)	(11.20)	10.58	(1.15)
PRIMROSE	A	10.25			1.35 x 7
	D		(11.45) x 5		
ROSEBERY	A		11.50		No. 7 Passenger Service must take preference.
	D		12.15 p.m.	11.22	
REN. BELL	A		12.45 x 7		Stations concerned to be on the alert for amended crossings should such be necessary.
	D		(1.15)	11.45	
ZEEHAN	A		1.45	12.10 p.m.	

UP

		No. 1 GOODS Monday Conditional	No. 3 GOODS Monday to Friday Inclusive	No. 5 ORE Mon. to Sat. Inclusive	No. 7 PASSENGER Mon. to Sat. Inclusive	No. 9 ORE Monday Conditional
		a.m.	a.m.	a.m.	p.m.	p.m.
ZEEHAN	D	6.15	6.15		12.50	
REN. BELL	D	(6.45)	(6.45)		1.14 x 4	
ROSEBERY	A					
	D	(8.0)	(8.0)		1.43	
PRIMROSE	A					
	D	(8.30)	(8.30)	(11.45) x 6-4	— x 8 Monday	(2.45)
FARRELL	A					
	D	(9.5)	(9.5)	(12.20) p.m.	2.7	(3.10)
BOKO	A	9.45 x 2-4-6-8	9.45 x 2-4-6			
	D	12.5 p.m.	10.40	(12.50)	2.25	(3.40)
GUILDFORD	A	1.55	12.30 p.m.	2.25	3.30	
	D	(2.15)	(12.50)	(2.40)	3.40	(5.30)
HAMPSHIRE	D	(3.15)	(1.50)	(3.40)	4.26	(6.30)
BURNIE	A	4.25	3.0	4.50	5.23	7.40

Times in parentheses are approximate only.

Road Motor to and from Waratah connects at Guildford with Burnie-Zeehan Motor in mornings only.

F. McCORMICK, Manager

ON THE MAIL

The early crew, having already prepared the loco and made up the train, departed Burnie yard and the crew for The Mail would be waiting outside the engine shed, where they jumped aboard 'on the fly'. This train departed at 6.30 am, and often didn't arrive back at Burnie until about 3 o'clock.

The Mail was always hauled by one of the Dübs engines, and was the mixed passenger and goods train which went right through to Zeehan. It carried passengers, livestock and perishables. Cattle, logs, pregnant women – you name it. This train stopped at most of the stations and little sidings along the way and shunted, so it was a slow trip. Milk and bread was unloaded at places such as Bulgobac and Renison Bell. The guard did most of the unloading and loading, along with the porters at the bigger locations such as Guildford, Primrose and Farrell, although the engine crew pitched in and helped at times.

Burnie crews ran the Down Mail as far as Boco – about the halfway point – where we'd change over with the Zeehan crew and bring the Up Mail back to Burnie. Boco was normally as far as the Zeehan crews ran. 'Strahan Day' was Monday, Wednesday and Friday, when The Mail train from Burnie connected with the Strahan train, and then to the Queenstown train – so the train had to be on time at Zeehan. The same trucks could go right through from Burnie to Queenstown if required, and some trucks went all the way from Hobart through to Queenstown. Certain days on The Mail were stock days, when we'd pick up livestock all along the line – pigs, cattle and sheep. They never had refrigerated trucks back then, so the animals were carted live right through to Queenstown to be killed and butchered.

LEFT: 1957 EBR Working Timetable. ~ Peter Ralph collection

RIGHT: In May 1963, the twilight of the EBR steam era, Beyer Garratt No. 12 storms out of Primrose with a northbound ore train. ~ Weston Langford

PAGES 56&57: An ASG loco approaches Guildford during an April 1962 snowfall. Stored rail motor No.5 can be seen to the right of picture, while at left are several EBR fettler's houses. ~ Keith Atkinson, Train Hobby Publications

20A

ON THE FOOTPLATE

Some of the old blokes were pretty tough to fire for in this era – you wouldn't dare back chat 'em! We had some good drivers, and we had some hard drivers. I worked with one old bloke, Wilfred Summers, who was pretty raw on the Garratts. One day a fireman said, 'Wilfred, you're killing me.' 'How'd you make that out?' he said. 'I need puff today – puff tomorrow's no bloody good to me.'

The Beyer Garratts' fireboxes were so big you could stand up inside them. When we were cleaning the tubes out and so on, my cap would just touch the top of the box – that's how deep they were. The Beyers initially had one fireman, and he'd have to shovel up to twelve tons of coal per day. This work was often too much for the men, and firemen actually fainted through exhaustion on two occasions. Following this, the crews kicked up such a stink that the company had to put on two firemen.

There were four Dübs engines in total, 6, 7, 8 and 11, and they all steamed well. I worked on the Dübs a few times, and they were bloody hard work. If you had a good driver and good coal you were all right, but if your driver liked to use a lot of steam, you were in for a hard day.

At Christmas time they'd pull the rail motor off and put on a Dübs. I was on with Jimmy Norton-Smith for four days straight one Christmas on passenger trains. We ran the Dubs the 88 miles from Burnie to Zeehan and back again, all in one shift. They were long days – Jimmy nearly killed me! The Dübs locos had long, narrow fireboxes, but when they were steaming hard, you only fired the back of the box anyway. After we arrived at Zeehan we'd take coal and water, then turn the loco on the wye and oil up. This left about a half hour before we had to head off again to Burnie. 'Come on, quick', Jimmy would say, 'we'll go over to the Federal Hotel for a couple.' This was just a stone's throw from the station. The old publican, Bernie Walford, would see us coming and he'd have two pots sitting on the bar waiting. Smithy would have three or four beers, then we'd go back over and I'd start shovelling to get the fire hot so she wouldn't be green.

LEFT: ASG No. 20A hauls the *West Coaster* over Pieman River bridge on 1 February 1963. ~ Weston Langford

Jimmy would turn the peak of his cap up, and 'Right Away.' 'Shwoosh' – he'd open that regulator right up and we'd go charging out of the station. On one of those Christmas shifts we were going down into the Ring River, when my nose started to bleed badly. Then it started pouring. I showed Jimmy. 'What have you done?', he said. He had to take over the shovel and fire going up the hill out of the Ring, and later on he said to me, 'You made your nose bleed on purpose, didn't you!' Jim was one of the characters, but they were all good blokes, just the same.

Only a few crews worked the *West Coaster* train – brothers Jimmy and Dickie Norton-Smith, Laurie Milburn, Sid Young and Gary Lowry. The train only ran for a few years, and it finished not long after the road was put through between Guildford and Rosebery. We jokingly called this train the 'Blue Flyer' – although it only went at about 30 mph! None of the Dübs engines ever ran again after this train was put off.

The ASGs were great engines, and gee they'd go if you had good coal! A good load of coal made for an easy day. I was on an ASG with old Reg Flight coming into Bulgobac one day. He was a bad-tempered old bastard, although he was really a good bloke all the same. You could row with him today, and tomorrow he'd shake hands with you! You always knew when Reg was getting wild, because you could see him going red from the shirt up to his felt hat. I said, 'Eh, Reg, what's wrong with it?' 'What'd you mean what's wrong with it?', he growled. 'Come and have a look at this back engine', I said, 'it don't look right to me.' I wasn't seeing things – the rear cylinder was cracked down through the bolt holes and right through the frame. This had occurred more than once, and they'd been patched up several times already.

THE LUNCH TIN

One time I was firing for Reg on a Garratt. We were going up the hill at a fairly good pace of about 8 mph, so Reg thought he'd have his lunch. But he'd no sooner opened his lunch tin when the engine started to slip and play up, so he promptly closed his lunch tin and shut off the regulator as quick as he could and applied sand. He got the engine settled down again and reopened his lunch tin, but no sooner had he done this than once again, the engine started to slip and carry on. This time Reg really lost his cool. He grabbed his lunch tin and hurled it straight into the firebox and said 'There – you may as bloody well have it!'

THE RUN TO PRIMROSE

At 6.00 am every morning except Sunday, the empty ore train departed Burnie and went through to Primrose. This train was normally hauled by one of the Beyer Garratts. When you left Burnie, as a fireman you were 'into it' right away, and you didn't put your head up until you reached the five mile point, when the grade eased off a bit. We stopped and took water at Ridgley, which was about 10 miles out, and we again took water at the 32 mile tank, just north of Guildford, and then again at Bulgobac. Then it was undulating most of the way through to Guildford. From Guildford it was fairly flat country through Hatfield to the top of Que Hill, and from here it was all downhill to the Pieman River, then a short uphill section before going down the Bobadil to Primrose. 25 mph was the line's speed limit.

The train normally arrived at the EZ company mine at Primrose at about 10 o'clock, and you'd go in and cut your van off and let it run into the wye, then shove the empties in the siding. After that you'd go to the coal stage, where it was 'head down arse up'. Then you'd clean the fire, oil up, have tucker, and come back and put your loaded train together. The driver did a brake test and you'd leave around midday.

When you left Primrose to come back home, you had to go up the Bobadil, which was only a short grade but it was very steep and was mostly in cuttings, so the rails were always greasy. We used a lot of sand through there. The trouble was when you left Primrose with a full load, you only had saturated steam available to you, as the superheated steam didn't come in until the engine got really hot. You didn't have any run up, so these trains were lifted with great difficulty. You needed a full head of steam before you left Primrose, with the needle right on the red mark, and full gauge glasses. Then as you came over the top of the hill near the Pieman River bridge, you started shovelling. When the fire was nice and hot and everything was ready, you'd cross the bridge and you'd be into her – regulator wide open. It was a 1 in 40 grade up to Boco, about four miles away.

Later, the Bastyan Dam was built, and the track was deviated a few hundred yards to the west, and a new big concrete bridge was built over the Pieman River. The old bridge was left intact and it, along with the old formation, is well under water.

From Boco it was flat running to Bulgobac tank, where we'd stop to take water. After you took water, you'd build your fire up for the four mile climb up the Que Hill and on to Hatfield. After this you only had the short climbs out of Guildford and Ridgley to contend with – the rest was all downhill running. It was about a six hour trip home – we'd get back to Burnie around 6 o'clock. We'd dump our load in the yard, before turning the loco on the wye, and then we'd go over the pit to knock the fire out and sign off.

SAFEWORKING

The EBR ran on the Train Staff and Ticket safeworking system, and the staff stations in my time were Burnie, Hampshire, Guildford, Boco, Farrell, Primrose, Renison Bell and finally Zeehan. The first train through the section ran on the ticket, and following trains ran on the ticket or staff with a 'Notice of Train Ahead' attached – a note stating that 'such and such train left Burnie at this time and has not yet reported at Hampshire', which was twenty miles away. So when you were on a following train, you had to keep a good look out ahead in case the train in front had stopped in the section. On more than one occasion this system resulted in a Garratt loco running into the guard's van of the train in front! In the winter time it was often still dark when the early morning train departed, so you had to look for the lights on the back of the van. You'd just see two little red dots in the gloom. In the fog we had to watch out more.

There were many instances when trains got stuck. One time Bruce McCaskill left Primrose with an ASG, and I was driving a Beyer. We had the staff, as we were the last train out. We got down to the Bobadil, and I called out 'Hang on.' I saw poor old Mick Lucas, the guard, standing up on the bank, and he had the longest stick he could find with a red flag on it. The next thing we knew the detonators were going, and here was Bruce stuck down in the Bobadil. Bastard of a place it was. We got out and I said, 'What's going on?' Bruce said 'We're stuck here – can't get out.' Neil Townsend was our guard, and he came up to see what was going on. I said 'Unhook me and I'll give you a push.' So I got onto the back of the van and I shoved him out onto what we used to call Bungaree Straight. I leathered him out of there and off he went. 'Well', I said, 'we won't see him again today', as we went back down to get our train. Then, bugger me dead, when we came up to the 62 mile tank, here he was – stuck again. So we gave him another nudge. We caught him again at Bulgobac, and I said, 'now he's gone', but then at about the 51 mile we caught up to him again. So we gave him another push, but he got away from me a bit around a curve, and I couldn't see much with the steam, so the next thing – 'CRUNCH' – we ran into the van, and I stoved it in pretty bad. When we hit,

Mick Lucas came flying out of that van so fast I don't think he even touched the running boards – he looked like he was treading on fresh air! I'll never forget him standing there shaking his head, saying, 'Me van, me van – look what you've done to me van!'

Their train got away eventually, but soon after this episode a notice appeared stating:

UNDER NO CIRCUMSTANCES IS ONE TRAIN TO PUSH ANOTHER

This notice was signed by the manager. Then not long after, another train became stuck. A telephone was attached to the telegraph wires and a call was put through to Burnie, with the question 'What are we going to do?' Fred Bartly said, 'Push him.' 'But it's out on the notice', said the driver, 'you're not allowed to push a broken down train.' 'Bugger the notice', said Fred, 'Just get him out of the road.'

THE ARGENT TUNNEL

I had a few stints as fireman and driver at Zeehan. On the way back from Zeehan the running wasn't too bad, although there was a bit of a grade out of the Ring River up to Renison Bell. We always made sure we put on a good fire well before we reached the Argent tunnel, so it would be burnt out before we went through, and we didn't cop too much smoke in the cab. By gees it got hot in there on a Beyer.

At one point in the 1950s there were a lot of New Australians – 'foreigners', we called them – in camps, working on the track. They were Germans and Czechoslavakians, Austrians, the lot. The cook would always come running out when we came through, yelling out 'Coal! Coal!' So we'd throw out a few good lumps. One day I was on with Geoff Brown on a Beyer, and we went charging into the Argent tunnel, and here's all these foreigners looking at us. Browny laughed and said, 'They reckon we're not going to fit, mate!' And it was true – some of them were in a panic, pointing towards the tunnel, and it really must have looked like we'd get stuck, because that tunnel was very tight.

EBR Morris inspection car at Farrell Junction in January 1961.
~ Keith Atkinson, Train Hobby Publications

NO GUARD

We went without the guard once. We were spreading ballast on our way down the Que Hill, and were running on the ticket through McCarty's cutting. I looked back and saw someone waving from the lookout in the guard's van, and I thought they had finished and were giving us the 'Right Away', so off we went. We got to Bulgobac, where we had to shunt a couple of trucks of chaff for the mill horses. 'Gee', said the driver, 'the guard's taking a bloody long while – go and round him up.' So I went back, and the carpenter from Guildford was in the van. I said, 'Where's the guard?' He said, 'You left him behind.' So I did the shunt.

When we arrived at Boco, the Zeehan mob were there waiting for us, and I said to the Zeehan guard, 'You better come with us to Primrose.' He said, 'Where's your guard?' 'Buggered if I know', I said, 'we left him up the scrub!' So off we went, and of course our guard caught the next Down train and met us later.

THE DIESELS

In total the EBR employed about fifteen loco crews in the 1950s. When the diesels were brought in, many of the crews were put off. Management, in their wisdom, decided to start combining trains and running them with nine locos at once. This saved on crews in theory, but it was eventually realised that if anything went wrong, there were only two locos in the Burnie sheds to help out. Then they took the guard's vans off, so the guards had to ride in the back loco. This arrangement only lasted about twelve months, before they took the guards away all together, and there was a big stink about that.

In 1992 they wanted to bring in one man crewing. I said, 'I've been on this line my whole bloody life, and I've had rain, hail, snow, trees and rocks on the track, I've seen everything – one man on the loco is no good to me. So I called it a day. Then in 1997, at the age of 68, they bought me back to do the EBR Centenary runs with Don River Railway's steam locos.

RIGHT: For a period in the 1980s, the EBR ran long trains with multiple 10&11 class locomotives, hauling ore concentrates from Melba Flats and Primrose. In November 1987, locomotive 1106 and eight other diesels round this classic set of curves on the downhill approach to Burnie. ~ Peter Ralph

LEFT: Thick snow on the Hellyer branch. ~ John Watkins, Burnie Regional Museum

In 1988, the 11½ km spur line was built from Moory Junction, south of Guildford, to the mine at Hellyer. Construction of the new railway took just nine months, and the line was officially opened on 10 April 1989.

The ore reserves at the Hellyer mine were estimated to be 15 million tons of silver-lead-zinc, with excavation having begun in 1985. About 360,000 tons of ore was hauled annually on this new line, until its closure in June 2000.

EBR
EBR

LOCOMOTIVES OF THE EMU BAY RAILWAY

A variety of steam and diesel locomotives saw service on the Emu Bay Railway during its century of operations. From the days of the Van Diemen's Land Company, with their underpowered Hunslet 4-4-0s, to the introduction of the massive Beyer Garratt locos in the 1930s, to the beginning of diesel locomotion in the early 1950s, the EBR employed a unique array of motive power.

A variety of rail cars also saw service on the EBR, providing economical passenger and mail service, and reducing the number of costly loco hauled trains. A number of motor cars were also converted to run on rails, used as inspection vehicles and even as an ambulance. The company also hired motive power at times, from both the Mount Lyell Railway and the Tasmanian Government Railways.

BEYER GARRATTS

To handle the expected traffic from the new Rosebery mill, in 1930 the EZ company bought three large Beyer Garratt locomotives from Manchester, England. Their arrival at the railway coincided with the onset of the Great Depression, and the dwindling traffic meant the new locos were not required. Following a series of trials, they were put in mothballs until traffic picked up in 1936, at which time they were placed into service, providing a massive improvement in hauling capacity.

The 132 ton Beyer Garratts were the workhorses of the company for many years, but were known as 'man-killers' due to their large fireboxes. Such was their hunger for coal that two firemen were required to operate them for much of their service life. Following their withdrawal from service by 1963, the three Beyer Garratts were unmercifully cut to pieces and sold off for their scrap metal value. This hard-nosed decision reflected the unfortunately common attitude in Australia of callously erasing our history and discarding, one by one, the stepping stones of our progress.

UPPER RIGHT: One of the new 132 ton Beyer Garratt locomotives at Burnie, following delivery and assembly in 1930.

LOWER RIGHT: A Beyer Garratt was involved in this spectacular runaway train wreck near Brooklyn Road crossing in Burnie. 18 July 1950.
~ Both images Burnie Regional Museum

DÜBS

Four of the Dübs 4-8-0 locomotives, Nos. 6, 7, 8 and 11, operated on the EBR, and when introduced they were the most powerful locomotives in Tasmania. The first three locos were purchased from Dübs & Co. Locomotive builders of Glasgow, Scotland, and they arrived at Burnie in 1900. The fourth engine, which arrived in 1912, was built by the North British Locomotive Company, which had taken over Dübs in 1903.

In 1960, two of the Dübs engines, No.6 and No.8, were dressed up, fitted with smoke deflectors and painted blue for the new *West Coaster* service which ran until just after the Murchison Highway was put through the West Coast in 1963. They were also named after prominent West Coast mountains, respectively *Murchison* and *Heemskirk*.

Two of the four engines escaped the scrapper's torch. *Murchison* became a static display at Zeehan's West Coast Heritage Centre. And in 1978 *Heemskirk*, after a decade rusting in the salt air at a Burnie seaside park, was transported to the Don River Railway at Devonport, where it was lovingly restored to operating condition. Following its return to service in 1996, the restored Dübs was the centrepiece of the EBR's 1997 centenary celebrations.

RIGHT: *Heemskirk* takes water at Bulgobac whilst running the *West Coaster* in November 1962.
~ Bernie Kelly

AUSTRALIAN STANDARD GARRATTS

Five of the much-maligned Australian Standard Garratt locomotives were operated by the Emu Bay Railway. All were second hand. The ASGs were hurriedly designed and put together in 1942 for the war effort, and as such had a number of design flaws which were to irreparably tarnish their reputation. These problems were considered so bad that the locomotives were effectively 'black banned', with engine crews in Queensland and Western Australia refusing to operate them. In an attempt to rectify the design flaws, EBR workshop staff – already experienced with Garratt locomotives – made a number of modifications, and after the teething problems were sorted out, the ASGs were considered a great success.

Three of the ASGs, Nos. 16, 17 and 18, were obtained from Queensland between 1948 and 1953, and the other two, Nos. 20 and 20A, came from the Tasmanian Government Railways in 1961 and 1962. Numerous modifications were carried out in the EBR workshops, including wheel flanges being fitted to the leading drive wheels, the addition of steam powered reversing gear, improved regulator handles, enlarged sandboxes, improved smokeboxes and firebox doors, the fitting of cylinder drain cocks and improved lubrication methods, along with many other alterations.

Engine crews preferred working the ASGs to the Beyer Garratts, as they were more comfortable and consumed less coal. ASG No. 20 ran away to its destruction near Burnie on 20 February 1962, and was scrapped. It was replaced with an ex-TGR Garratt, numbered 20A. The eventual fate of the ASGs was the same as that of the larger Beyer Garratts, with all succumbing to the scrapper's torch in the mid 1960s.

ASG SPECIFICATIONS

BUILT: 1943-1945
TOTAL PRODUCED: 57 – Clyde Engineering in New South Wales (22), Newport Workshops in Victoria (13), Islington Workshops in South Australia (12) and Midland Workshops in WA, (10)
WEIGHT: 116 tons (fully loaded)
LENGTH: 85 ft 10 in
WHEEL ARRANGEMENT: 4-8-2+2-8-4
GAUGE: 3 ft 6 in
MAXIMUM BOILER PRESSURE: 220 psi (180 psi on the EBR)
COAL CAPACITY: 6 tons
WATER CAPACITY: 4,200 gal
CYLINDERS: (4) 14 in diameter x 24 in stroke
DRIVING WHEEL DIAMETER: 4 ft
TRACTIVE EFFORT: 34,520 lb

RIGHT: ASG 17 at Guildford in April 1962. ~ Keith Atkinson, Train Hobby Publications

C 17

THE DIESEL ERA

The EBR's first foray into the world of diesel locomotion was in September 1953, when the company took delivery of an 0-8-0 Paxman Voith diesel hydraulic loco. PVH1 (later re-classified as No. 21) was built in 1953 by the North British Company in Glasgow, Scotland, and was one of the first mainline diesel hydraulic locos to operate in Australia. After overcoming various teething problems, the efficient engine considerably reduced running costs on the line.

Following the success of PVH1, three Paxman V-12 diesel hydraulic locomotives were ordered from Walkers of Maryborough, Queensland. Known as the 10 class, they arrived in 1963, and were an immediate success. From this point on, the transition from steam to diesel traction occurred rapidly, with the remaining steam locomotives being withdrawn from service by 1966. An additional 10 class locomotive appeared on the railway in that year. Then in December 1969, the first five of the 11 class locos were delivered from Walkers. The 11 class were powered by Caterpillar V-12 diesel engines, and all were in traffic within a month. Two more followed in March 1971, making a total of seven in the class.

The introduction of the diesel locos changed the railway forever, with more efficient operations possible. It also meant improved working conditions, and the long, hard days filled with dirty, labour intensive work became a thing of the past. The thundering, fire-breathing, steaming monsters pounding their way along the tracks provided unforgettable sights and sounds to those who witnessed them, and their passing was mourned by many. By modern standards, the iron horse may have been labour intensive and inefficient, but it is difficult to imagine an invention of greater value.

By mid-2000, the four 10 class locos had become surplus to requirements and were stored at Burnie. They were retired in 2001, and were pensioned off to various Australian tourist railways. In March 2002, all vacuum braked stock on the railway was phased out and replaced with air brake stock, resulting in the faithful old 11 class locos being withdrawn from service – their last run taking place on 23 March 2002. All seven members of the class were subsequently sold to rail operators in Queensland.

PVH1 loading a classic Pioneer 'Scenic Clipper' coach at Rosebery, in January 1963.
~ Keith Atkinson, Train Hobby Publications

Loco 1103 derailed at Highclere. 16 January 1990. ~ Burnie Regional Museum

Locomotives 1102, 1105, 1001 and 1103 haul a concentrates train through Boco on a typically bleak West Coast day. February 2000. ~ Bernie Kelly

LEFT: EBR plate on locomotive 1001.

RIGHT: Concentrates train crossing the tannin-stained Ring River in March 1998.

BELOW: Driver Sid Young speaks to the Traffic Controller in Burnie, whilst the train crosses Ring River bridge.
~ All images Peter Ralph

RIDING THE RAILS

The author's first experience of the old Emu Bay Railway was a visit in June 2000. Upon making enquiries at Burnie's railway offices, I was hastily informed that the last train ever to the Hellyer mine – and a steam-hauled passenger train at that – had just departed...'Gee, I dunno mate...maybe a couple of hours ago.' 'WHAT?!' A mad drive into the hilly countryside above Burnie followed, but as the car shuddered to a halt at Moory Junction, the last of the carriages could just be seen disappearing into the bush! Oh well, at least I'd *seen* a train on the Hellyer branch.

Then, having read of its former importance, I decided to visit the old junction station at Guildford, with the hope of finding a few substantial railway remains. Unfortunately, this freezing, windswept location proved something of a disappointment, with practically all trappings of its former status having been ruthlessly eliminated. Worst of all, this included the station building, which once contained a famous refreshment room complete with a log fireplace, hot pies and scones! But, other than the sound of the wind in the nearby tree tops, all was quiet at Guildford. And then it began to snow...

On a return visit to Tasmania in March 2002, I was very fortunate to make a memorable journey along the old EBR, just prior to the retirement of the reliable 11 class locos and the end of the vacuum brake era. The adventure involved a pre-dawn start at Burnie. After meeting the driver, I clambered up into the warm cab of the 11 class. With a flurry of windscreen wipers and violent wheelslip, our train load of empties departed Burnie in driving rain – so typical of the West Coast – and soon we were charging up the 1 in 33 grades towards Ridgley. Later, with the rain temporarily behind us, the sun appeared and illuminated a scene of magnificence, with pockets of mist in the valley floors and lush green pastures of the farming districts. The train snaked its way along the sinuous track, with rabbits darting here and there and horses, cows and sheep taking fright and bolting across their paddocks. Smoke drifted up lazily from the odd farmhouse chimney.

The old junction station of Guildford came and went, and then the rails entered the dark, mysterious forests which characterise much of western Tasmania, with gushing creeks and rivers too numerous to count. Then, while descending the Que hill, we came across the bizarre sight of a wrecked log train – a tangled mess of twisted steel and splintered logs – scattered down an impossibly steep ravine. I was told that about 80 metres of track had been damaged in this episode, although the locos had somehow stayed on the rails. The rest of the train was adjudged too expensive to recover and had apparently been abandoned – possibly for all time!

Then the rain began again – heavy, soaking rain, and I spared a thought or two for the men who surveyed and built the line, and the many who followed in their footsteps to operate and maintain it. Now, the bush was uninhabited. Refreshments were strictly BYO on this adventure, as we passed through lonely, remote country without a hint of civilization for the most part. One of the trip's highlights was the crossing of Lake Rosebery. The train seemed to lunge out into space, rumbling high above the swirling, tannin-stained waters far below. The train reached the outskirts of Rosebery at the Primrose loading facility, where we shuddered to a halt. Before long the empties were shoved in the appropriate siding, and loading of the zinc concentrates, or 'calcines', commenced in very efficient fashion. No mucking about on this railway, I thought. 'The sooner they're loaded, the sooner we'll get home' stated the driver matter-of-factly.

Eventually, loading was complete and the train was remarshalled, and without further ado, we commenced our return trip to Burnie – this time with the four blue locos straining under the load of heavily laden ore trucks. The long uphill grind from Lake Rosebery was memorable, with regular wheelslip on the greasy rails, the driver making constant use of the sanding equipment. Progress became so slow that stalling seemed a distinct possibility, but the locos held on, and the train eventually topped the grade. We emerged from the woods and ran through picturesque North Coast farming country. The train then began winding its way downhill towards the old port of Emu Bay, and before long we came to an abrupt halt in Burnie's cold and windswept railway yard.

Only another week or so remained for the seven reliable 11 class locos, which were to be be replaced by Tasrail locomotives. It was the end, too, for the vacuum brake rolling stock, with conversion to air brake looming. It felt like the end of an era, with the relics and memories of the proud old Emu Bay Railway being swallowed whole by the dreaded but inevitable modern world.

LATER YEARS

In 1940, the ten mile branch line from Guildford Junction to Waratah – the original railway to the Mount Bischoff tin mine – was closed, with traffic having dwindled following a large reduction in output from the mine. In 1965, services between Rosebery and Zeehan were also discontinued, with road transport having consumed most of the traffic on offer. Financial hardship was to plague the EBR right through the years of its operations. The constant need to upgrade the permanent way and rolling stock, along with costly repairs to damaged bridges and earthworks, coupled with erratic metal prices and the 'boom and bust' nature of mining, made demand for traffic inconsistent.

In February 1967, the EBR was formally taken over by its main customer, the Electrolytic Zinc Company of Australia. A major boost to traffic occurred in 1970, when a new loading facility was built at the location of Melba Flats, twelve miles from Rosebery, to which concentrates from the Mount Lyell mine were trucked. This loading was a result of the Mount Lyell smelter being closed, with concentrates railed to Burnie, then shipped to Japan for processing. A heavy rejuvenation project was undertaken on this section of track, which had been disused since 1965 when the line beyond Rosebery was abandoned.

The route of the EBR was altered on several occasions, most dramatically in 1978 with the construction of the Bastyan Dam north of Rosebery. These works required a two mile track deviation and the erection of two new bridges, and resulted in the famous old Pieman River bridge being abandoned, soon to disappear under the chilly waters. Another deviation was required in 1985, with the expansion of the Pieman Dam near Renison Bell. This development saw the construction of a new concrete bridge spanning the Ring River, which replaced the previous tall structure. Heavy loads of bulk cement and explosives were carried for these hydro schemes.

Until 1983, passengers were able to travel on the mixed trains which had a passenger carriage attached, but after this date the carriages were sold off, and intending passengers had to make do with a ride in the guard's van. In 1990, the running of regular goods trains was discontinued, and much of the line's character disappeared with them. From this time, the railway became a true bulk carrier, carting only concentrates and logs. In the early 1990s, guards were removed from trains, and driver only operations took effect in December 1994.

Don River Railway diesel locomotive Y6 arrives at Melba Flats, after hauling an enthusiast special from Burnie in May 1999. ~ Peter Ralph

The EBR celebrated its centenary in 1997, with the running of a series of steam excursions along the line arranged by the Don River Railway. Newly restored Dübs No.8 *Heemskirk* was the star of the show. In 1998, the EBR was taken over by ATN – Australian Transport Network – part of the Wisconsin Central company which operated Tasrail. So, after more than a century of independent operations, the old EBR was finally absorbed into Tasrail's rundown network.

Today, the old Emu Bay Railway lives on, known blandly as the 'Melba line', just another part of Tasmania's skeletal railway system.

North Mount Farrell Tramway

Officially called the North Mount Farrell Tramway, but known variously as the Farrell Tram, the North Farrell Tram or the Tullah Tramway, this 2 ft gauge railway was possibly the 'quaintest' of the many iron roads to grace Tasmania's West Coast. The line ran from Farrell Junction on the Emu Bay Railway to the isolated mining town of Tullah, a journey of 6½ miles.

Silver-lead mining began at Tullah in 1899, with the ore initially being carted out by packhorse – a profit-ruining arrangement. With the arrival of the Emu Bay Railway through the district, an eight mile horse-drawn, wooden-railed tramway was put through to Boco siding, which was constructed in just four months and opened in 1902. As mining operations increased, this primitive tramway was replaced by the aforementioned 2 ft gauge steel tramway.

A total of five steam engines operated over the line during its life. The best known was a Fowler loco which arrived in 1924, named *Wee Georgie Wood* after a popular British actor and comedian of the times. It was joined some years later by another Fowler, a similar engine named *Wee Mary Wood*. Other engines consisted of an ex-Magnet Tramway Orenstein and Koppel loco, which dated from 1901, and two Krauss locos were used at different times during the life of the tramway, one of which was built in 1892, and the other an ex-Mount Lyell engine dating from 1908. After a hard working life, *Wee Mary Wood* was withdrawn from service and cannibalised for parts to help rebuild an ailing *Wee Georgie Wood*.

The North Mount Farrell Tramway was a successful venture, hauling ore tonnage far in excess of the timber-railed tramway it replaced, and the line remained in operation into the 1960s. It was beloved by locals, and was truly the lifeblood of Tullah, as in addition to mining produce and inbound materials, the tramway carried all passengers in and out of town, along with building products, perishables, groceries, mail, and most importantly, beer for the pub!

The much-loved locomotive, *Wee Georgie Wood*, an 0-4-0 Fowler built in 1924. This sturdy workhorse weighed just 5½ tons, and burnt either wood or coal. The little engine pounded the light rails between Farrell Junction and Tullah for 40 years.
~ Burnie Regional Museum

Wee Georgie Wood on the North Mount Farrell Tramway following a heavy snowfall. ~ Burnie Regional Museum

A Ride Behind Wee Georgie Wood

Peter Ralph

Towards the end of its tenure, the little line had become quite famous, and something of a tourist curiosity. Many rail enthusiasts and historians from Tasmania and around Australia ventured to the tramway to experience a ride though history. One such enthusiast who visited Tullah during this period was Victorian Peter Ralph.

In November 1957, I ventured to the West Coast of Tasmania for a trip along the famed North Mount Farrell Tramway. I caught the Emu Bay Railway train to Farrell, from where I went on a fascinating trip behind *Wee Georgie Wood*. This was a tiny engine which ran along the quaint 2 ft gauge tramway, the only transport to the isolated mining township of Tullah – a place which had no road access whatsoever.

This tramway ran to a timetable and connected with the Up and Down EBR trains. When our train pulled in, *Wee Georgie Wood* and its two carriage train was made up and ready, already loaded with produce for the Tullah store and mine. The driver was the only crew member to be seen, and I have no memory of ever being asked to buy a ticket. It was certainly a very casual affair! A handful of passengers climbed into the basic little carriage, and the mail bag off the Zeehan train was swung aboard. Then with a toot on the shrill whistle and a jolt, we took off around a sharp two chain curve, and headed for Tullah.

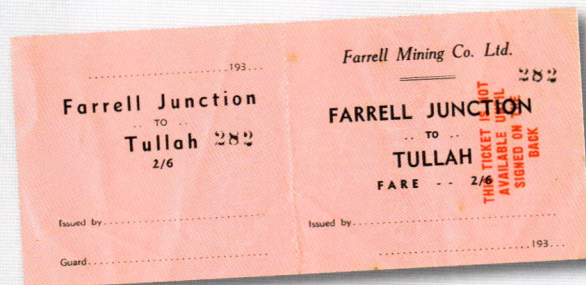

The scenery was most picturesque, but the journey was a bit rough. *Wee Georgie Wood* and the two little carriages bucked and swayed along the track, and at times the speed seemed little faster than walking pace. After an hour or so, we arrived at the little hamlet of Tullah, where the passengers were deposited and the produce and goods were unloaded. Tullah was like something out of a Wild West movie. It was a quaint and isolated place, with a few dilapidated looking buildings here and there, and the remoteness made it unique. Some of the townsfolk turned up to meet the train's arrival, perhaps waiting to greet a passenger, or possibly in the hope of receiving a letter or parcel. They were typical Tasmanian country folk – very friendly and hospitable.

The driver took *Wee Georgie Wood* off and ran it around the wye so as to face funnel first on the return journey. After a quick turnaround, the engine was hooked back on, and I reboarded the carriage for the journey back to Farrell. I was the only passenger! A little way along the track we stopped on a bridge, where a stream gurgled below, and here the driver dropped a hose into the drink to take water for the little engine. We eventually arrived back at the junction station at Farrell, just in time to catch the rail motor to Burnie.

........193...
Farrell Junction
.. TO ..
Tullah 282
2/6
Issued by........
Guard........

Farrell Mining Co. Ltd.
282
FARRELL JUNCTION
.. TO ..
TULLAH
FARE -- 2/6
Issued by........
........193...

ABOVE: Ticket to Tullah. ~ Don River Railway

LEFT: *Wee Georgie Wood* at Farrell Junction, with an interesting load for Tullah. February 1960. ~ Keith Atkinson, Train Hobby Publications

RIGHT: *Wee Georgie Wood* at Tullah. ~ Train Hobby Publications

Krauss No. 9 at Farrell Junction, as an Emu Bay Railway ASG shunts the yard. 4 January 1957. ~ Ray Bruce, Neil Tate collection

It has been said that all good things must come to an end, and the end for the North Mount Farrell Tramway came when a road was belatedly put through to Tullah, connecting it to the modern world, as it were, in 1962. This spelt the end for the tramway, which quickly became superfluous to the town's requirements, and services to Farrell Junction were discontinued.

Wee Georgie Wood continued working trains around the Tullah mine until 1964.

ABOVE: *Wee Georgie Wood* at Tullah in May 1963. ~ Weston Langford

RIGHT: *Wee Georgie Wood* shunting ore wagons at Tullah mine in 1964. ~ Bernie Kelly

Rosebery and the Electrolytic Zinc Company

Rosebery main street in March 1964. ~ Bernie Kelly

The town of Rosebery, named after British Prime Minister Archibald Primrose, the 5th Earl of Rosebery, grew from humble beginnings in 1893 to become one of the larger population centres on the West Coast.

In 1893, a body of zinc-lead ore was discovered at Rosebery, but early mining was hampered by a lack of transport to a suitable smelter. In August 1899, the Emu Bay Railway arrived, connecting the town with the port at Burnie. The line was extended south to Zeehan the following year, which allowed access to the smelting works located there. In 1916, the Electrolytic Zinc Company of Australasia Pty. Ltd. was formed, and the products of this company were to become crucial to the success of the Emu Bay Railway, which hauled the ore concentrates to Burnie.

In 1927, the EZ company announced plans to build a large new mill at Rosebery, accompanied by a railway spur siding. The expected heavy increase in traffic to Burnie required upgrades to the Emu Bay Railway's motive power, and three large Beyer Garratt locomotives and new wagons were purchased by EZ and leased to the EBR. Wharf facilities at Burnie were also upgraded. In 1930, the Great Depression caused a slump in demand, and it was not until 1936 that the mill began healthy production.

Over the following decades the EZ company went from strength to strength, with ever expanding operations and increasing output. The company also continued to employ modern technology, with increased mechanisation and efficient work practices.

Zinc-lead mining continues to this day at Rosebery, in what has become one of the longest running and most successful mining operations in western Tasmania.

UPPER RIGHT: EZ Company buildings at Rosebery, 1939.
~ Galley Museum, Queenstown

LOWER RIGHT: Aerial ropeway at Rosebery in January 1971. The warning sign advises people not to stop or loiter beneath the ropeway! ~ Peter Ralph

EZ Company Ruston shunter hard at work at Primrose in November 1962. ~ Bernie Kelly

The Hercules Haulage, a 2 ft gauge self-acting incline tramway, transported ore from the Hercules mine to the railhead at Williamsford until 1929, when an aerial ropeway was constructed to Rosebery. The haulage operated until February 1985, with the aerial ropeway to Rosebery also meeting its demise in that year.

UPPER and LOWER LEFT: The top of the haulage. Workers were conveyed up the haulage in a passenger carriage. ABOVE: The car arrives at the foot of the incline after a ten minute descent. January 1971. ~ All images Peter Ralph

ZEEHAN – SILVER TOWN

Zeehan Main Street in November 1962, with a few fading reminders of its past glories. ~ Bernie Kelly

Interest in the Zeehan area was first aroused in the early 1880s, following the discovery of tin at Mount Heemskirk, but it was the silver deposits found later which cause the greatest excitement. When the railway from Strahan reached the bustling town in 1892, Zeehan was considered to be on the verge of a silver boom to rival that at Broken Hill in New South Wales. By 1900, over 100 mining companies were operating in the district, and a network of tramways had been built around the town. Zeehan's population was approaching 8,000 inhabitants, making it the third largest town in Tasmania, behind only Hobart and Launceston.

Flushed with wealth, the town boasted its own stock exchange, along with many fine and elegant residences, businesses and hotels and an opulent theatre called The Gaiety – Australia's largest at the time. The mining boom was short lived however, and by 1910, the town's silver-lead deposits were running out. It turned out that the field was quite shallow, and any mines sunk deeper than 300 ft rarely found payable ore bodies. By 1920, Zeehan's fortunes and population were in a steep and permanent decline.

STRAHAN-ZEEHAN RAILWAY

This 3 ft 6 in gauge line was part of the Tasmanian Government Railways, and extended from the harbour at Strahan, running some 28½ miles north to Zeehan. Construction of the railway was a frustrating and expensive affair, with heavy earthworks in places and numerous bridges, and costs amounted to over £200,000 by the time it was completed.

The official opening took place on 4 February 1892, but the line was seemingly given a low priority by the government, as a motley collection of second hand engines and ramshackle rolling stock was delivered to Strahan for use on the line, much to the consternation of locals. In October 1900, the line was extended a further 1½ miles around Macquarie Harbour between Strahan and Regatta Point, allowing trains to connect with the newly opened Mount Lyell Railway from Queenstown. This link, combined with the completion of the Emu Bay Railway from Burnie through to Zeehan one year later, meant that a passenger could finally complete a train journey from Queenstown right through to Burnie, changing trains at Regatta Point and Zeehan.

In stark contrast to the spectacular view from the train window on most West Coast railways, the Strahan-Zeehan line was not endowed with scenic delights, as it ran mainly through scrubby country, punctuated by a few sand dunes. Various newspaper reports from the early period of the line's operation are sprinkled with 'less than kind' reports from passengers. Despite the criticism, the line saw healthy traffic, but the arrival of the Emu Bay Railway soon put paid to that, and a steady decline began. The line was reportedly in a dreadful state by the end of WWII, with a succession of derailments resulting.

Victorian rail enthusiast Peter Ralph, then only a teenager, has mixed memories of travelled on the Strahan-Zeehan railway. His trip along the line was made in January 1953, as part of a journey from Queenstown to Burnie, and from his account it appears not much had changed since the 'bad old days'...

> Upon arrival at Regatta Point on the Abt railway, we crossed to the opposite platform and boarded the ramshackle looking Tasmanian Government Railways train for the journey to Zeehan. This train was hauled by loco CCS25, attached to a couple of battered old carriages and a guard's van.
>
> The rain was torrential as we departed Strahan, and before long the roof of our carriage began to leak quite badly, and we had to change seats several times in order to try and stay dry. When we arrived at Zeehan, I cheekily asked the Station Master if I could have a discount due to the poor condition of the train. This request didn't impress the SM too much. 'No', he replied abruptly, 'you can't have one.' And that was that!

The Strahan-Zeehan railway was losing money and patronage, and it eventually closed on 2 June 1960. Most of the line was soon dismantled, with much of the formation being used as the foundation for a new road linking the two towns.

DUNDAS LINE

The 7½ mile railway from Zeehan to the mining town of Dundas, and the terminus further on at Maestris, was opened in 1892. It was built to tap the mining wealth expected from the flourishing Dundas area, and was operated by the Tasmanian Government Railways, working as an extension of the Strahan-Zeehan railway. In 1899, as part of the agreement to access Zeehan, the Emu Bay Railway was forced to purchase the line. The EBR had no wish to run trains to Dundas, so for the next three decades, the EBR maintained the permanent way while the TGR ran the trains. The mining boom at Dundas came and went, and train services, which had mostly run at a loss, were cancelled in 1929. The rails of the Dundas railway were lifted for scrap in 1940.

EBR rail motor No.8 at Zeehan in 1957. ~ Frank Kelly, Bernie Kelly collection

TASMANIAN GOVERNMENT RAILWAYS.

No.

TRAIN STAFF TICKET.

TRAIN No.________

To the Engine Driver.

YOU are authorised, after seeing the Train Staff for the Section, to proceed from

WEST STRAHAN

to

STRAHAN WHARF

and the Train Staff will follow.

*Signature of Person in Charge*________________________

*Date*____________ [OVER.

ABOVE: TGR Train Staff ticket for the West Strahan to Strahan Wharf section.
~ James Smith collection

RIGHT: The delightful tourist town of Strahan, pictured in April 1957. The Hamers Hotel forms the centrepiece of the main street, and the shiny rails of the Tasmanian Government Railways Zeehan line skirt Macquarie Harbour.
~ Peter Ralph

E. M. LUTTRELL
DRAPERY CLOTHING AND FOOTWEAR
E. M. LUTTRELL

NORTH EAST DUNDAS TRAMWAY

The North East Dundas Tramway was a seventeen mile 2 ft gauge railway, which ran from Zeehan to Williamsford. It was built and operated by the Tasmanian Government Railways to access the rich mining fields in the Mount Read area. The narrower gauge of this line resulted in an inconvenient break of gauge at Zeehan, as the government line to Strahan was of the Tasmanian standard 3 ft 6 in gauge. Critics were quick to point out the costs involved in the transhipping of goods, etc, but the fact remained that the construction of a wider gauge railway through such rugged country would have been prohibitively expensive.

Construction commenced at Zeehan in 1896, with the line opening in stages, finally reaching Williamsford by June 1898. Zinc lead ore from the Hercules mine reached the wagons of the North East Dundas Tramway at Williamsford via a mile-long, 1,642 feet tall, 'self acting' tramway, which had a maximum gradient of 1 in 1.5.

The North East Dundas Tramway was successful in its early years, carrying heavy ore trains from Williamsford to the smelters two miles to the south of Zeehan, and also carrying a healthy number of passengers, as the railhead was less than five miles from the growing settlement of Rosebery.

LEFT: Garratt locomotive K1 – the world's first such loco – storms around one of the line's many sharp curves, this one near Montezuma Falls. ~ Burnie Regional Museum

RIGHT: A Sharp Stewart locomotive on the North East Dundas Tramway. One of the most fabulous scenes on any Australian railway was this curved trestle bridge at Montezuma Falls, the spray from which sometimes saturated passing trains following heavy rain – a not-infrequent occurence on Tasmania's West Coast. ~ Peter Ralph collection

The extension of the Emu Bay Railway through to Zeehan in 1900 put paid to most of this passenger traffic, but the line continued to carry a high volume of ore until the outbreak of World War I in 1914, when the Zeehan smelters were closed. From this time on, ore traffic was greatly reduced.

The North East Dundas Tramway's magnificence was described glowingly as being unsurpassed in Australia. The railway cut its way through the ranges, via deep cuttings and over timber bridges, then crossed a steep gully within sight of Tasmania's highest waterfall – Montezuma Falls – on a large trestle bridge. At its highest point, the line climbed to an elevation of 1,550 ft above sea level, a rise of more than 1,000 ft from Zeehan. Grades as stiff as 1 in 25, combined with impossibly tight reverse curves, made for difficult operating conditions, and an unusual variety of motive power was employed to work the line. This included two Krauss locomotives and two Sharp Stewart locos, one of which suffered a catastrophic boiler explosion in 1899 at Zeehan, killing both the driver and fireman.

In 1900, an unusual looking German-built Hagans J class loco arrived at Zeehan. This 42 ton loco was immensely powerful, but its weight caused numerous derailments and damaged the lightly laid track, and it was not a great success. In 1910, two Beyer Garratt locos, K1 and K2 – the first Garratts to operate anywhere in the world – arrived at Zeehan. The 0-4-0+0-4-0 articulated compound Garratts were well suited to the winding narrow gauge line, and they saw service for more than two decades.

In 1929, the EZ company in Rosebery constructed an aerial ropeway to transport ore from the Hercules mine to their smelters, rendering the North East Dundas Tramway obsolete. Train running ceased, and the line was officially closed in 1932.

WILLIAMSFORD
DEEP LEAD

LEFT: A Sharp Stewart locomotive heads a North East Dundas Tramway train at Williamsford, formerly known as Deep Lead. c.1900. Note diamond crossover in the yard. ~ Burnie Regional Museum

ABOVE: K1 Garratt locomotive at Zeehan. ~ Don River Railway

Upon closure of the North East Dundas Tramway in 1932, the famous K1 Garratt remained in storage until 1947, when it was donated by the Tasmanian Government to its maker, Beyer Peacock & Co. Ltd in Manchester, England.

Here it was cosmetically restored and put on display. Beyer Peacock closed in 1966, and K1 was saved by the Ffestiniog Railway in Wales, and from 1976 until 1995 it was displayed at the York Railway Museum.

In anticipation of the reopening of the Welsh Highland Railway, K1 was restored to operating condition, and it entered traffic in 2004. During restoration, it was found that K1 contained many of K2's parts, including boiler and main frames, although the main engine unit frames, including the cylinders, belonged to K1.

QUEENSTOWN & MOUNT LYELL

A ground for the toughest of footballers! Queenstown's famous gravel sports oval, as seen in June 1961 with a well-attended match between the Gormanston Blues, in the navy blue and white guernseys, and the Lyell Maroons in the maroon and yellow. The Lyell Maroons went on to win the 1961 Queenstown Football Association's premiership. ~ Frank Kelly, Bernie Kelly collection

The story of Mount Lyell is one of the great chapters in the history of Australian mining. At its peak, the wealth which flowed from this 'Mountain of Copper' made up no less than a third of Tasmania's entire export earnings.

The Mount Lyell region was first probed for precious metals in 1862, when the Tasmanian Government commissioned geologist Charles Gould to venture into the wilds of the West Coast, in the hope of finding mineral deposits to exploit. He found little of value, although he did name Mount Lyell during his travels. In 1881 Cornelius Lynch, an Irishman, was in charge of a prospecting party which ventured from Hobart Town. Lynch discovered gold in a tributary of the Queen River, which he named Lynch's Creek, and as news spread a frenzy of gold panning began.

Then in 1883, another party were prospecting at Mount Lyell, when they discovered gold near a rocky outcrop they called the 'Iron Blow', believed to be the source of all the region's alluvial gold. Modest quantities of payable gold was won from the area, and before long fortune seekers were scouring the Linda Valley and the surrounding hills, hoping to strike it rich. Fortunes were won and lost, but most departed worse off than when they arrived. Life was tough for these West Coast pioneers, who tramped through the muddy and almost impenetrable forest, living rough on basic rations, all the while being pounded by the never ending rainfall for which the region is famous. It has been said, after all, that on the West Coast it rains for nine months, and then the wet season begins!

THE MOUNT LYELL MINING COMPANY

The Mount Lyell gold petered out, but then the real source of the Iron Blow's wealth – copper – was discovered by two mining men, Bowes Kelly and William Orr, who had become wealthy on the booming silver fields of Broken Hill. In 1891 they purchased the failed gold mining syndicate, realising they were buying a copper mine, and in 1892, the Mount Lyell Mining Company was formed. In 1895, a brilliant German American metallurgist, Robert Sticht, was engaged by the Mount Lyell Company, and his experimental process of extracting copper from the local ore was a tremendous success, winning the company international acclaim. By mid 1896, a large smelter had been erected and was in operation, belching out great clouds of sulphurous smoke.

The Mount Lyell self-acting haulage, which carried ore from the Iron Blow mine. The 2 ft gauge tramway at the bottom of the incline was serviced by Krauss locomotives, which transported ore to the smelter. The wooden sign proclaims 'DANGER – NO THOROUGHFARE'. ~ Galley Museum, Queenstown

PENGHANA AND QUEENSTOWN

A ramshackle settlement called Penghana – Welsh for 'head of a valley' – soon sprang up around the base of the smelting works. This rough and ready collection of company buildings, shacks and tents, was swept by wildfire in December 1896, and was abandoned in favour of a new township a mile down the valley – Queenstown. The quintessential mining town, Queenstown soon boasted a population of 5,000, all of whom either worked for the Mount Lyell Company or depended upon it in some way. No less than fourteen hotels sprang up, catering to the thirsty miners. One can only imagine the scenes in Queenstown during the heyday of mining and railway operations, with the flurry of activity around the mines and the screeching of steam whistles.

Working conditions were hard in the early years. Unions were weak, and the bosses were said to have had hearts colder than stone. The men often worked seven days per week, moving thousands of tons of rock by manual labour, using picks and shovels which they were obliged to purchase before they could start work. With the smelters belching out a continuous cloud of sulphurous fumes, Queenstown became almost permanently enveloped in a murky fog. Townsfolk complained they could taste sulphur in their mouths, and that it caused nose bleeds. Everything in the valley became coated in a fine coppery powder, and even the household firewood gathered from the surrounding hillsides burnt with pretty green flames.

Before long, with much of the timber being cut down for firewood, and the effects of the constant noxious fumes, the hills surrounding Queenstown became denuded of vegetation, made worse by erosion and bushfire. This unhealthy situation continued until 1922, when a new flotation method of ore treatment began. The process eliminated much of the sulphur from the air but created a new problem. Now, vast amounts of mine tailings were being dumped into the Queen River, and these found their way downstream into the King River and out into Macquarie Harbour, clogging the waterways with a thick grey sludge, and creating an environmental disaster of monumental proportions.

LEFT: With its eleven blast furnaces operating, by 1899 Mount Lyell's smelter was in full production, presenting a scene of great industry.
~ West Coast Heritage Centre, Zeehan

NORTH LYELL

At the same time as the Mount Lyell Mining Company was busy expanding their operations on the western side of the Mount Lyell ridge, Irishman James Crotty was busy creating another copper empire on its eastern side. Crotty arrived on the West Coast in 1879, and in 1884 he purchased a third share of the Iron Blow. In 1888, he and several other men began the ill-fated Mount Lyell Gold Mining Company, and he and Bowes Kelly had become bitter enemies following its underhanded acquisition in 1892. Then in 1897, Crotty began a new company called the North Mount Lyell Copper Company. He wasted no time developing his mine, building a smelter, and putting a railway connection through to Kelly Basin on Macquarie Harbour. The townships of Gormanston and Linda grew rapidly, with the total population of the district matching that of Queenstown's.

Under the shrewd leadership of Bowes Kelly and Robert Sticht, the Mount Lyell Company had developed superior smelting practices, but mined inferior quality ore, whereas the North Mount Lyell Company mined superior ore, containing up to 35% copper. However they but were unable to capitalise upon it due to their inferior smelter, with their troubles being compounded by gross mismanagement, much to the consternation of disgruntled British shareholders. An amalgamation of the two companies was the glaringly obvious solution, and after much resistance, the marriage of convenience finally occurred in August 1903. This saved both companies from liquidation. The new company, now armed with a combination of high quality ore, skilful smelting practices and clever management, turned Mount Lyell into one of the world's great copper mines.

NORTH MOUNT LYELL RAILWAY

Opened in 1900, the North Mount Lyell Railway was put through from the Linda Valley to Macquarie Harbour. Initially, a 2 ft 6 in gauge railway was surveyed, but the line was eventually built to the Tasmanian standard of 3 ft 6 in. The line was well built, with the final cost amounting to over £316,000, but construction progressed slowly, with allegations of corruption rife.

The terminus was at the town of Linda, connecting to the North Lyell Mine via a 2 ft tramway and an aerial cableway, and a short spur line also ran to Gormanston. From here, the 28 mile line ran in a southerly direction, at first over gentle terrain through open country. Intermediate stations were Crotty and Darwin. The line crossed the King River on a 160 ft steel bridge, before entering more difficult country, where grades as steep as 1 in 40 were required. Fantastic scenery was encountered in this mountainous section, with the rails following the fast flowing Bird River through thick rainforest to Macquarie Harbour. The alignment through the mountains required heavy earthworks, a tunnel and wooden bridges, but landslips were to prove a constant problem, necessitating a deviation and the removal of the tunnel. On Macquarie Harbour, a railway station and yard, along with locomotive workshops and other railway facilities were located at Kelly Basin, with the main wharf a further mile around the shore at Pillinger.

The line officially opened for business in December 1900, with the spur line to Gormanston opening in 1901. A smelter was built at the township of Crotty, but this was to prove an embarrassing failure, and it was closed by 1903. Rolling stock on the North Lyell was extravagant, with three luxuriously appointed saloon type carriages, containing both first and second class accommodation. Three Avonside locomotives were imported from England, and three geared Shay locomotives were obtained from the USA, intended for the company's ill-fated Comstock line which was never completed. Other than goods and mixed trains, the railway had a regular passenger service which coordinated with the shipping timetable, meaning passengers could travel from Linda or Gormanston through to Strahan via Kelly Basin in a matter of hours.

The railway lost a fortune from day one, exacerbated by mismanagement and extravagance, and in 1903 it was taken over by the Mount Lyell Mining and Railway Company. Following the amalgamation, the populations of Crotty and Darwin dwindled – with townsfolk abandoning their dwellings and moving away in search of work – and train services were greatly reduced.

From this time, the line was mostly used to haul timber, as well as seeing the occasional picnic train, and a rail car was introduced to handle mail and the few remaining passengers. The old North Mount Lyell Railway lingered on for twenty years, until being closed in stages between 1924 and 1927, with the rails being pulled up by the end of the decade.

SS *Kawitiri* at Kelly Basin, c.1900. ~ West Coast Heritage Centre, Zeehan

Shay No. 5 locomotive hauling ore at the North Lyell mine.
~ Burnie Regional Museum

The town of Crotty presents a prosperous scene in 1900. In the foreground can be seen North Lyell Railway's Avonside locomotive *DJ MACKAY*, and in the background, the Crotty smelters belch fumes into the sky.

Upon the amalgamation of the two rival mining companies of Mount Lyell in August 1903, Crotty's population rapidly dwindled, and by the 1990s the town's remains had disappearred altogether under the waters of Lake Burbury.
~ West Coast Heritage Centre, Zeehan

The Mount Lyell Mine Disaster

Tasmania's worst mining disaster occurred on the morning of Saturday, 12 October 1912, deep inside the North Lyell mine. At 8 am on that fateful day, 170 men entered the North Lyell shaft to begin work in six underground levels. A couple of hours later, the smell of smoke was detected, and it was discovered the pump house at the 700 foot level was on fire. Most of the miners kept working, as they considered the fire would burn itself out, but suffocating smoke began drifting through the various shafts and drives. Many of the men did not become aware of the danger until it was too late. As the smoke thickened, groups of miners were brought to the surface in the cage, eight at a time, but many others were trapped by smoke and deadly carbon monoxide fumes.

By evening, the families of trapped miners keeping a vigil on the surface were confronted with a sinister column of smoke pouring out of the mine shaft. 95 men were still missing.

A Mighty Rescue Effort

Distress calls were made, and rescue trains were quickly sent from Hobart, Launceston and Devonport. Meanwhile, men and equipment were dispatched from the Victorian mining towns of Ballarat and Bendigo, and before long two steamers – the *Lady Loch* and the *Loongana* – left Melbourne and dashed across the heaving seas of Bass Strait, headed for Burnie. The *Loongana* famously made the crossing in a record time of 13 hours 35 minutes. The men and rescue equipment from these ships were immediately transferred to a special train waiting at Burnie – a loco and single carriage – and it rushed off towards Zeehan at great speed. Waiting at Zeehan was an Abt locomotive, which then raced the carriage through to Queenstown. The train dashed through Strahan at a rapid pace, with police waving people out of the way. The train made the journey from Burnie to Queenstown fully five hours quicker than normal – a time never again bettered.

Meanwhile, teams of men had continued their rescue attempts throughout the Sunday and into Monday, but smoke and fumes severely hampered their efforts. Hopes for the missing men were further dimmed when rescuers began finding the bodies of dead miners in the stifling depths.

At the 700 ft level, a pathetic note was found attached to a mine timber:

> 'Seven hundred level. North Lyell mine, 12-10-12. If anyone should find this note convey to my wife. Dear Agnes - I will say good-bye. Sure I will not see you again any more. I am pleased to have made a little provision for you and poor little Lorna. Be good to our little darling. My mate, Lou Burke, is done, and poor old V. and the driver too. Good-bye, with love to all. Your loving husband, Joe McCarthy.'

A long rope was lowered down the main shaft of the mine, and late on the Monday afternoon, men at the surface were surprised to receive a message from below: 'Men to go to the surface.' Then a little later, another signal: 'Men at the 1,000 ft level.' When the rope was hauled up, a handkerchief wrapped around a tobacco tin was attached to it. Inside the tin was a pencilled note:

> '40 men in 40 stope. Send food and candles at once. No time to lose. J. Ryan'

Supplies were hurriedly dispatched down the shaft, giving hope to the forlorn group of mothers and wives desperately awaiting news at the surface. But the situation underground was becoming desperate, and later another note was received, stating:

> 'We have had enough. Losing confidence.'

On the Tuesday morning, another note was sent up the shaft:

> 'Try and get us as soon as possible. The cold is terrible and there is none of us well. We are depending entirely on the compressed air. If that fails we are done.'

Shortly after the rescue train's arrival at Queenstown on the Tuesday afternoon, two men – a local miner and a Melbourne fireman – were fitted with smoke helmets and lowered to the 1,000 ft level, where they found a group of very relieved and happy miners. It was Wednesday morning before the men were assisted in climbing up 160 ft of slippery ladders to a point from which they were hauled to the surface in a large bucket, and 4½ days after entering the North Lyell mine, the last of the survivors emerged.

A TERRIBLE DEATH TOLL

Attempts to retrieve the bodies of the men in the 600, 700 and 850 ft levels, where the smoke was known to be at its deadliest, proved impossible due to the continuing fire, and the mine was sealed and partially flooded. It was not until December that men again entered the mine, to discover the full extent of the tragedy. Some of the dead were found standing at their drills, or laying down as if asleep, with others sitting against a wall as if in idle conversation with other miners. The bodies were retrieved one by one, and it was not until June 1913, eight months later, that the last of the deceased was finally brought to the surface. A series of mournful funeral processions passed along the streets of Queenstown, and a pall of grief fell over the tight knit community.

In all, 42 men were killed in the Mount Lyell disaster, with several additional survivors later succumbing to the effects of carbon monoxide poisoning. The tragedy remains the fourth worst mining disaster in Australia's history. Today, a large boulder excavated from near the North Mount Lyell shaft serves as a monument in Queenstown's cemetery, where the men were buried side by side – a stark reminder of that dreadful event of a century ago.

J. BAWDEN
V. BIANCHINI
W. BOLTON
J. BOURKE
S. BRAY
L. BURKE
J. CREEDON
C. GREEN
J. DAVEY
T. GAYS
H. GUY
J. HALL
E. HILLS
W. HORNE

J. JENKINS
W. JONES
J. LEEMAN
Z. LEWIS
J. Mc CARTHY
E. Mc CASLAND
T. Mc CULLAGH
J. Mc GOWAN
B. Mc LOUGHLIN
A. Mc MASTER
T. MAHER
H. MITCHELL
P. MOORE
J. O'DAY

C. O'KEEFE
J. PARK
C. QUAK
P. REILLY
F. ROLFE
J. ROLFE
T. SAUNDERSON
L. SCOTT
W. SMITH
J. STUDWELL
J. TREGONNING
W. TREGONNING
R. TREVERTON
H. WRIGHT

The Mount Lyell mine disaster monument in Queenstown's cemetery. ~ Nick Anchen

THIS STONE FROM MOUNT LYELL STANDS AS
A LASTING MEMORIAL TO THE FORTY TWO
MEN WHO LOST THEIR LIVES UNDERGROUND
IN THE NORTH LYELL MINE FIRE ON 12TH
OCTOBER 1912 AND ARE ALL BURIED HERE

ABOVE: Inside the Mount Lyell smelter. March 1964.

LEFT: The Lyell Highway cuts through the desolate, denuded hills of Queenstown. 1962. ~ Both images Bernie Kelly

The Mount Lyell Railway

In the wilds of western Tasmania, a train ascends the 1 in 20 rack section of the Mount Lyell Railway, between Dubbil Barril and Rinadeena. The load consists of coke for the Mount Lyell smelter. November 1962. ~ Bernie Kelly

The greatest challenge confronting the newly formed Mount Lyell Mining Company was how to affordably transport their product to the coast. At first it was thought the construction of a standard adhesion railway would be possible, and in March 1893, survey teams set out to find a suitable route through the mountains. It was soon discovered, however, that the use of a conventional railway would be impossible due to the steep gradients required to cross the mountains. Different options for a railway were examined, one of which involved the boring of a great tunnel, an alternative deemed too costly. Eventually the construction of a cog or rack system was recommended as a workable solution, and the proposal was adopted.

A MAGNIFICENT ENGINEERING ACHIEVEMENT

In late 1894, construction had commenced on the most ambitious railway ever attempted in Tasmania, a fourteen mile route from the Mount Lyell mine to the King River port at Teepookana. Carus Driffield, a South Australian engineer who had built railways at Broken Hill, was placed in charge of the project. The Mount Lyell Railway would be built to the standard Tasmanian 3 ft 6 in gauge, and when completed was the steepest railway in Australia. The railway utilised the Abt rack and pinion system which had proven successful in the Harz Mountains in Germany, along with many other locations throughout the world.

Hundreds of men were employed for the mammoth task, with one team working south from Queenstown, while another worked north from Teepookana, on the King River. The men worked in dreadful conditions, building bridges and carving out the line with picks, shovels and wheelbarrows. After work, they went home to a wet canvas tent and poor food. Many of the workers quit due to the dreadful working and living conditions, and yet the remainder struggled on, building a railway which was nothing short of an engineering marvel.

Numerous deep cuttings and high embankments were required, along with 48 bridges, of which the 250 yard 'Quarter Mile Bridge' was the longest and most difficult to build. The piles for this huge structure had to be driven up to 20 yards through the silt before a solid base could be found. The bridge was 50 feet high, but despite this, floodwaters lapped just inches below the rails on occasions.

Rugged terrain in the King River Gorge. c.1897. ~ Galley Museum, Queenstown

The expansive 'Quarter Mile Bridge'. ~ Burnie Regional Museum

Busy Teepookana wharf in 1896. This unlikely port became Tasmania's fourth busiest, and with the frontier town's population quickly growing to 200, a school and a two storey hotel rapidly appeared. ~ West Coast Heritage Centre, Zeehan

The line was completed on 19 November 1896, in just nineteen months, at a total cost including rolling stock of £259,904. The first of the Abt engines had already arrived from Scotland in crates, and was assembled in temporary workshops at the remote location of Camp Spur. The new engine was tested on a short section of rack railway, and the Abt system was found to be suitable.

From Queenstown, the Mount Lyell railway ran along moderate ground to Halls Creek, before entering the Abt rack section for 1½ miles of 1 in 16 gradient to the summit at Rinadeena, 755 ft above sea level. From this point, the line dropped down a three mile 1 in 20 gradient of rack railway to the bottom of the grade at Dubbil Barril. The rails then followed the King River on relatively easy grades to Teepookana, where a port was established – this being the furthest point upriver where sizeable boats could navigate. Trains began running in 1896, with the railway's official opening being celebrated in typically lavish West Coast style on 3 April 1897.

Abt loco No. 3, driven by Peter Jack, at Regatta Point on opening day from Teepookana. 1 November 1899. ~ Abt Railway Society

The Mount Lyell company then extended the line a further five miles from Teepookana to Regatta Point, near Strahan, so as to gain access to superior port facilities, as well as connecting with the Government's Zeehan railway. This meant another crossing of the King River, at Teepookana, and for this purpose a large iron bridge was obtained from Scotland. It was delivered to the deepwater port at Strahan and floated up the King River on barges, before being winched into position.

The Teepookana-Regatta Point section opened on 1 November 1899, and once the Government line was connected a year later, the famous mining towns of Queenstown and Zeehan were linked by rail. One year later, when the Emu Bay Railway reached Zeehan, it became possible to travel by rail right through from Queenstown to Hobart – a dirty and uncomfortable 26 hour journey involving multiple changes of train.

THE PRIDE OF QUEENSTOWN

The railway was the lifeblood of the Queenstown community, and the Mount Lyell mine. Townsfolk congregated at Queenstown station to await the arrival of the trains, often to greet friends or relatives. These gatherings became a ritual, and the arrival and departure of the trains became the town's clock. Everything was carried by rail in these times, including the mail, perishables, groceries and the latest ladies' fashions.

The railway was a huge success, and business increased steadily through the years, in line with the Mount Lyell mine output. The railway became a large employer, with fettlers and other maintenance staff, train crews and shunters, station staff and fitters, many of whom were from the same family. At its peak, up to 25 men were employed at Regatta Point alone, including the unloading gang, as all the copper concentrates were manually shovelled out of the trucks by hand in those labour intensive times.

The annual Mount Lyell Company picnic trains to Teepookana, and later to Strahan, were a highlight on the West Coast calendar for many years, and were much anticipated by the children of Queenstown, as well as the 'railway kids' along the line.

On the appointed day, a procession of trains departed Queenstown, with families packed into converted coke and ore wagons, which in later years were fitted out with canvas roofs and temporary seating. After the day's festivities, which included foot races, wood chopping, tug-of-war competitions and much else, the trains returned to Queenstown, accompanied by a good deal of singing and frivolity. These picnics became a West Coast tradition, continuing right up until closure of the railway in 1963.

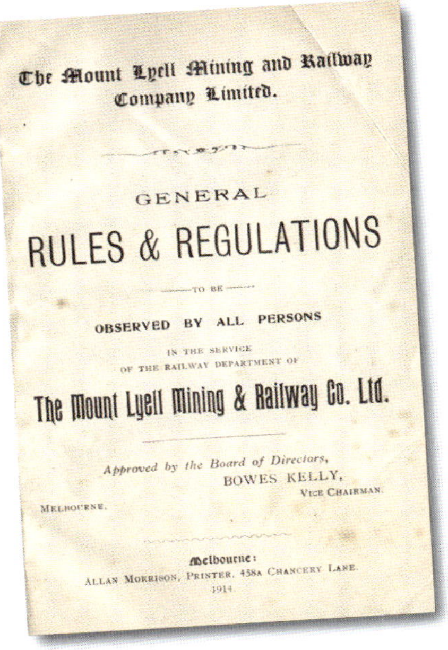

The Mount Lyell Mining and Railway Company Limited.

GENERAL

RULES & REGULATIONS

TO BE

OBSERVED BY ALL PERSONS

IN THE SERVICE
OF THE RAILWAY DEPARTMENT OF

The Mount Lyell Mining & Railway Co. Ltd.

Approved by the Board of Directors,
BOWES KELLY,
VICE CHAIRMAN.

MELBOURNE.

Melbourne:
ALLAN MORRISON, PRINTER, 458A CHANCERY LANE.
1914

ABOVE: Baldwin locomotive No. 3, about to depart Teepookana with the first Mount Lyell Company picnic train, on 5 December 1897. ~ West Coast Heritage Centre, Zeehan

LEFT: Mount Lyell Railway Rules & Regulations, dating from 1914. ~ Don River Railway

RIGHT: The arrival of Tasmania's Governor, Lord Gormanston, in 1897, attracted a huge crowd to Queenstown Railway station. ~ West Coast Heritage Centre, Zeehan

Locomotives of the Mount Lyell Railway

Abt loco No. 1 basks in morning sunshine in Queenstown yard. November 1962. ~ Bernie Kelly

ABT LOCOMOTIVES

The distinctive Abt locomotives became synonymous with the Mount Lyell Railway throughout its 67 year life. The company obtained four of these sturdy workhorses from Dübs & Co. Locomotive builders of Glasgow, Scotland. The Abt locomotives possessed both adhesion and rack engines, with two cylinders powering each. They were designed to haul 60 tons over the 1 in 16 and 1 in 20 rack sections of the Mount Lyell railway, and to retard the heavy trains going down the rack.

Abt No.1 entered traffic in late 1896, with Nos. 2-4 following between 1898 and 1901. The locos proved a tremendous success, and were much loved by their engine crews. In 1938, a fifth Abt loco was purchased from the North British Locomotive Company, which had taken over Dübs in 1903.

The Abt locos initially ran on the excellent Maitland coal, but later burnt a mixture of Tasmanian and Maitland coal, as an economy measure. Due to continuing problems in obtaining a reliable supply of steaming coal, the Abt engines were converted to burn oil in the late 1950s. Other modifications in this period included the fitting of electric generators and headlights.

ABT LOCOMOTIVE SPECIFICATIONS

BUILT: (Nos. 1-4) Dübs & Co. Locomotive builders, Glasgow, Scotland, 1896-1901
(No. 5) North British Locomotive Company, Glasgow, Scotland, 1938
TOTAL PRODUCED: 5
WEIGHT FULLY LOADED: (No. 1) 23 tons 14 cwt, (Nos. 2-5) 26 tons 4 cwt
TOTAL LENGTH: 22 ft 9¾ in
WHEEL ARRANGEMENT: 0-4-2
GAUGE: 3 ft 6 in
MAXIMUM BOILER PRESSURE: 175 psi
OIL CAPACITY: 440 gal
WATER CAPACITY: (No. 1) 440 gal, (Nos. 2-5) 600 gal
ADHESION CYLINDERS: (2) 11½ in diameter, 20 in stroke
RACK CYLINDERS: (2) 11½ in diameter, 15½ in stroke
DRIVING WHEEL DIAMETER: 3 ft
ADHESION ENGINE TRACTIVE EFFORT: (At 80% boiler pressure) 10,286 lbs
RACK ENGINE TRACTIVE EFFORT: (At 80% boiler pressure) 12,719 lbs

Regatta Point-bound train crossing the King River on Teepookana's large iron bridge. 15 April 1957. ~ Peter Ralph

Upon closure of the Mount Lyell railway in 1963, Abt No. 4 was broken up for parts, but the other four engines were preserved. Abt No. 1 was displayed at Zeehan's Pioneer museum. Abt No. 2 was placed on static exhibit at the Tasmanian Transport Museum in Glenorchy. Abt No. 3 was displayed in Queenstown at the 'Miner's Siding' park, near the former railway station. And Abt No. 5 was purchased by the Australian Railway Historical Society and was displayed at the Puffing Billy Railway museum at Menzies Creek, Victoria.

BALDWIN LOCOMOTIVES

In addition to the Abt locomotives, the Mount Lyell Company purchased three 27 ton, 0-6-0 tank engines from the Baldwin Locomotive Works in Philadelphia, USA. They arrived between 1897 and 1899, and were immediately pressed into service.

The Baldwins worked over the entire railway until the arrival of the four Abt locos, although they were limited in haulage capacity over the rack sections. They were also used around Queenstown, and in the 1920s were often seen shunting at Regatta Point.

By the 1930s the Baldwins were generally unused, and were stored out of service. Various unsuccessful attempts were made to sell them, and all had been scrapped by 1960.

RIGHT: Baldwin locomotive No.5.
~ Galley Museum, Queenstown

KRAUSS LOCOMOTIVES

A total of eleven 2ft gauge Krauss 0-4-0 locomotives were used by the Mount Lyell company on their 2ft gauge system. These consisted of 6½ ton, 7½ ton and 10 ton locos. A dual 2ft and 3ft 6 in gauge line ran from Queenstown station to the loco sheds and beyond. Several other lines fanned out to various parts of the Mount Lyell lease, carrying an array of building materials, firewood, coke, ore, limestone and silica, as well as mine workers. One line ran to the base of the main Mount Lyell haulage, a 2ft gauge self acting tramway which transported ore from the mine to the smelter over a steep ridge.

Another 2ft tramway ran five miles to the Lyell Comstock mine, north of Queenstown, and was built in 1913. This was a mountainous route which contained two zig-zag sections as well as several bridges spanning the Queen River, and a maximum gradient of 1 in 20. The line was abandoned in 1944 when mining ceased at Lyell Comstock.

Krauss locomotive No. 8 at Queenstown in January 1963.
~ Keith Atkinson, Train Hobby Publications

DS LOCOMOTIVES

The ageing Baldwin locos were replaced in the early 1950s by two ex-New Zealand DS tank locomotives, both of which had seen service on the New Zealand and later the Tasmanian Government railways. The DS class were obtained for the lower section of the line between Regatta Point and Dubbil Barril, as well as for use around Queenstown. They were withdrawn in the mid 1950s and were scrapped by 1959.

VULCAN DREWRY LOCOMOTIVES

Two 26 ton Vulcan Drewry 0-6-0 diesel mechanical locomotives were purchased in 1953. These engines developed 200 hp, and were pressed into service on the Regatta Point-Dubbil Barril section of the Mount Lyell Railway, freeing up the Abt engines for more intensive use on the rack sections.

RIGHT: Vulcan Drewry diesel mechanical locomotive, shunting at Regatta Point on a fine summer's day in January 1963.
~ Keith Atkinson, Train Hobby Publications

A Day on the Mount Lyell Railway

MICK MAXFIELD

Former Mount Lyell Railway engineman Harold 'Mick' Maxfield describes the operating conditions for drivers and firemen on the Abt railway. His fascinating memories paint a vivid picture of what was a highly skilled and sometimes unnerving job – operating trains safely up and down the steep and slippery rack sections.

Mick put pen to paper in 1998, when the Abt railway was on the verge of being rebuilt. The following is a description of a typical run from Queenstown to Regatta Point.

IN THE RUNNING SHED

The driver and fireman for the 7.45 am train arrive at the Queenstown running sheds at about 6.45 am, where they find their loco steamed up and full of fuel, water and sand. All moving parts on both the adhesion and rack engines have been oiled up and the whole loco cleaned – this being done by the night shift chargeman and cleaners. The driver does a quick check around the loco, then he and his fireman climb aboard and steam down to Queenstown station.

Their train is standing in the siding, already made up, loaded and weighed. They pull the train out and place it into the station platform, then run the loco around and attach it to the front. Depending on the number of passengers travelling, carriages from another siding are run down the incline and coupled up to the rear of the train by the guard and shunter.

After the vacuum brake hoses have been connected, the driver blows his brake to its 29 inches of vacuum, then puts the brake application lever into the running position. He then watches to see if the 29 inches of vacuum holds right through the length of the train. Any faults need to be rectified by maintenance personnel, and if the fault cannot be fixed, the offending wagon will be removed and replaced with another. Braking is crucial, as when descending the 1 in 16 and 1 in 20 grades on the rack sections, each wagon's brake has to hold its own weight, and any that do not place a burden on the rest of the train. Any two wagons not holding their weight could be the cause of a runaway down the grade. Once the driver is satisfied with the brakes, he gives his side rods, fly crank rod and cross heads another splash of oil and climbs back into the cab.

In the Queenstown running shed in May 1963. Abt No. 1 is on the left, and Abt Nos. 2, 3 and 4 are on the right. ~ Weston Langford

Queenstown yard in July 1963. Loaded ore wagons await dispatch to Regatta Point. ~ Michael Schrader, Train Hobby publications

By now it is 7.45 am, and the Station Master strides out of his office and gives the driver the all clear to depart. The fireman closes the adhesion exhaust column and adjusts the adhesion cylinder oil feed on the hydrostatic lubricator, then winds off the loco's handbrake and makes sure the cylinder release cocks are open. The driver blows the whistle, opens the adhesion regulator, and with a lot of hissing and clouds of steam, the little loco hauls its laden train out of the station.

Only a short steaming is necessary to get the train away, and the driver looks back along the train to receive the guard's all clear. After acknowledging this, he closes the regulator and blows the whistle for the first road crossing just outside the station yard. At this stage of the journey, the train is rolling on a downgrade, and the driver applies the brake to steady the train's speed where necessary.

On reaching Lynchford – a small station with just three or four fettlers' houses – the train stops briefly to allow the guard to telephone Queenstown and clear the section, then gain approval to proceed to Rinadeena. The train continues on, up the 1 in 40 grade to Halls Creek, where the 7.00 am train is waiting. The loco from this train will detach and help push the 7.45 am train up the 1 in 16 grade rack section to Rinadeena, at the top of the grade.

UPPER RIGHT: Mount Lyell Railway O class carriages at Queenstown in February 1960. Four of these luxuriously appointed cars were built by the Lancaster Railway Carriage and Wagon Company in England, between 1901 and 1902. ~ Keith Atkinson, Train Hobby Publications

LOWER RIGHT: A heavily laden ore train steams out of Queenstown, Regatta Point-bound, in November 1962. ~ Bernie Kelly

Mixed train running through the streets of Queenstown in November 1962. Note the thoroughly contaminated Queen River – the result of decades of pollution from the Mount Lyell copper mine. It has been estimated that over 100 million tons of mine tailings were dumped into these once-pristine waters, until the practice finally ceased in 1995. ~ Bernie Kelly

RIGHT: The steep 1 in 16 grade is evident in this splendidly composed image of Rinadeena – the top of the rack. May 1963. ~ Weston Langford

The Abt rack and pinion system was invented in 1882 by Swiss inventor Carl Roman Abt. The system consisted of a pair of toothed centre rails, attached to the sleepers between the adhesion rails, which meshed with toothed cogs on the locomotive pinion wheel.

A feature of the Abt system was that one tooth was always engaged in the centre rail and this, combined with regular traction from the locomotive's adhesion wheels, made the system particularly safe and efficient.

ENTERING THE RACK

When the train approaches the rack section, the driver has two choices. The first is to enter the rack rail tongue very gently with the rack engine in the stop position, and let it mesh into the rack entry rail. The beginning of the rack is tapered and set on springs, allowing the rack pinion cogs to mesh properly, which makes quite a 'clunking' sound.

The second method is to reduce the train's speed to about 2 or 3 mph. The driver then closes the rack engine exhaust column, while the fireman opens the release cocks on both the rack and adhesion engines to release any water build up in the cylinders, then starts the rack engine cylinder oil lubricator.

The driver starts the rack engine, well before the train has reached the rack entry. He then judges the revolutions of the adhesion engine and gradually brings the rack engine up to about 2.3 revolutions to the adhesion engine's one revolution. With this method, the loco quite often enters the rack rail without making a sound. The driver then gradually opens the rack engine regulator and notches up on the reversing wheel, shortening the valve stroke on both engines, thus saving steam and water in the boiler.

UP THE 1 IN 16 GRADE

By this time the loco from the 7.00 am train has come up behind the 7.45 am. The driver gives one loud whistle to let the lead loco driver know that he's about to start pushing, and the lead driver pops the whistle to acknowledge. This effort certainly doesn't go unnoticed, as the crew on the lead engine can really feel the rear loco pushing!

The fireman by now has the fuel oil valve and the atomiser valve well and truly open to keep a full head of steam, 175 psi. He then closes the cylinder release cocks. The fireman's side water injector remains on all the way up the grade, to keep the water level up in the boiler. Occasionally the driver puts his injector on if the fireman's does not hold. If the rails are greasy, both driver and fireman work their sand levers to stop the adhesion engine slipping, although one technique employed by some drivers is to regulate the flow of sand by admitting a very fine trickle all the way up the grade. Other than this, nothing more is to be done, so the crew sit back and let her climb the grade. Upon reaching the top, the fireman turns off the hydrostatic oil feed, then eases the oil fire back to idle, prior to the driver shutting the rack and adhesion engines off. The blower valve is then turned on to maintain a vacuum in the smokebox.

At Rinadeena, the train pulls up level with the overhead water hose, and the pushing engine returns to Halls Creek. It is always the fireman's job to top up the water tanks and sand boxes, if any sand has been used coming up the grade. Sand is crucial for safety while descending the rack sections, and it needs to be as dry as sand in an hourglass. A supply of dry sand is available at various places along the line; Halls Creek, Rinadeena, Dubbil Barril and Regatta Point. Most importantly, the fireman then tests the sand delivery pipes on both sides of the loco to ensure the sand is running freely before the loco commences its descent down the 1 in 20 grade to Dubbil Barril. Blocked sand pipes are normally cleared by giving them a good whack with a hammer.

Meanwhile, the driver checks and oils the rack and adhesion engines, including the axle boxes, and then walks along his train looking for any leaking brake cylinders. Back inside the cab, he puts the brake application lever into the blow off position until he gets it as high as it will go, past the 29 inches of vacuum until it shows 31-32 on the loco's vacuum gauge. By this time the guard has rung Queenstown to gain clearance for the Rinadeena-Dubbil Barril section.

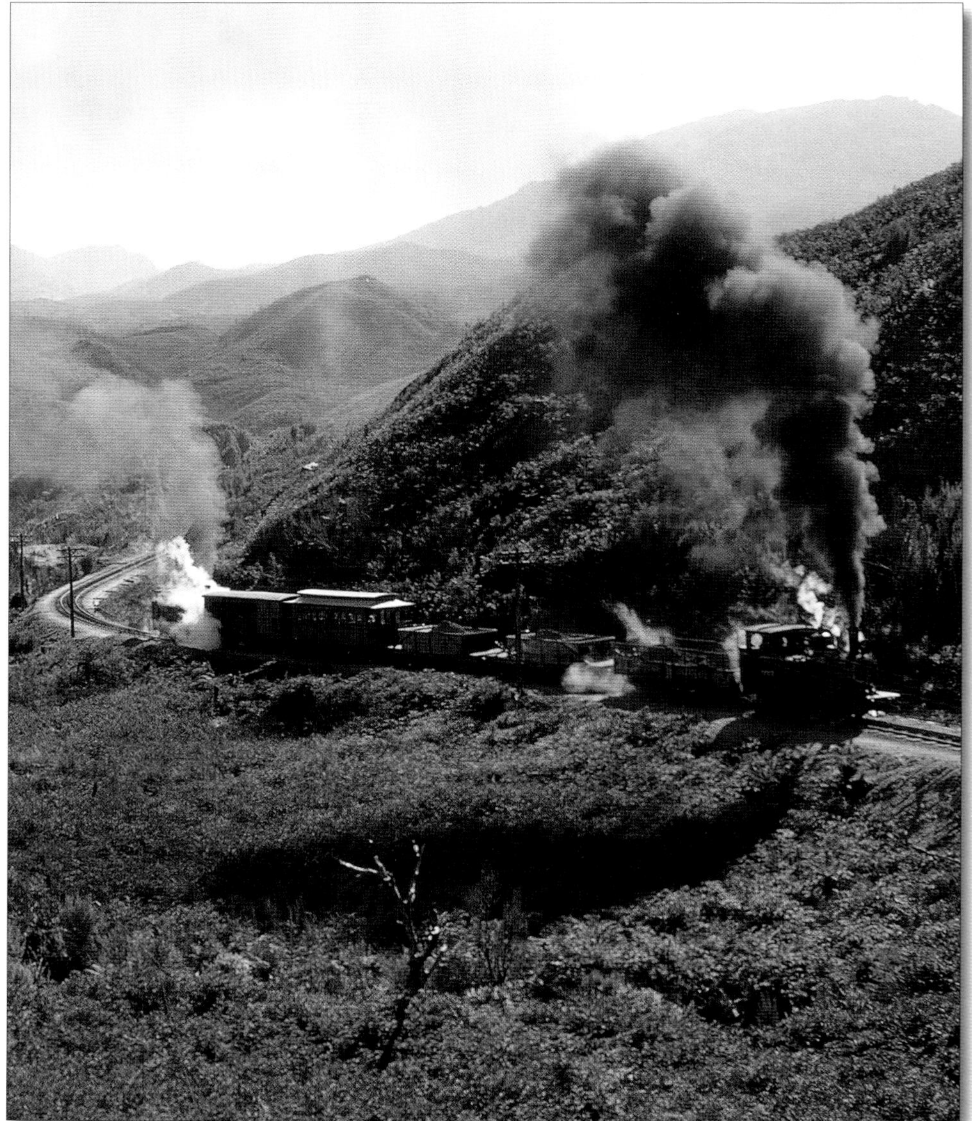

Pounding up the rack, from Halls Creek to Rinadeena. November 1962.
~ Bernie Kelly

Drifting down the rack to Halls Creek. ~ Bernie Kelly

DOWN THE 1 IN 20

The driver then sounds the whistle, closes the adhesion exhaust column and opens the adhesion regulator, and the train starts towards the 1 in 20 grade rack rail section to Dubbil Barril. As the train approaches the 'brow', the driver might be asking himself what sort of run he can expect down the hill today. Upon entering the rack, the driver closes the adhesion regulator, then opens both the rack and adhesion exhaust columns. He then opens the small release valve to the loco's vacuum brake cylinders, before releasing the vacuum brake on the loco only, and then opens the air flapper valve to the cylinders. Next he opens the rack and adhesion water valves which admit water to the cylinders to cool and lubricate the pistons and rings, and then winds back both the adhesion and rack engines into reverse. The loco is now holding itself with the counter-pressure brake. Next, the driver begins admitting air into the vacuum pipe along the full length of the train, thus actuating the brakes on all the wagons and carriages. The vacuum gauge in the loco's cab drops from 31 inches of vacuum to about 22 inches of vacuum, and he feels the train steadying nicely. Today's train has a good brake.

Some days the rail is nice and shiny from the previous day's traffic, but on other occasions it rains all night and the rails end up with a wet, rusty film on their surface. While descending the rack on greasy rails, it can feel like an ice rink with steel wheels on steel rails, as the train speed increases. It is best to keep all the wheels turning while braking rather than having them lock up, and this is where sand is useful. Skidding wheels can cause flats on the tyres, which is an expensive and time-consuming business to remedy, as the wheels need to be removed and either turned on a lathe or fitted with new tyres.

If the brakes are working well, the train may come to a complete stop on one of the curves, and this gives the driver a chance to blow his brake back up as high as possible. If the brakes do not hold and the train starts to run away, the driver sounds two loud whistles, and the fireman and guard both jump down and start applying handbrakes on all the wagons, but thankfully this is only an occasional occurrence, and may simply be caused by the types of wagons which make up a particular train.

DUBBIL BARRIL

When the train arrives at the bottom of the rack at Dubbil Barril, the driver closes the flapper valve, then the release valve on the loco's vacuum brake, before winding the rack and adhesion engines into forward gear. The fireman then opens the rack and adhesion cylinder release cocks. The driver blows the vacuum brake off the train and rolls out of the rack rail, pulling up level with the water tanks. He then proceeds to oil up the adhesion engine's moving parts plus the axle boxes, and checks the wheels, big ends, side rods and bearings for any signs of overheating. The fireman tops up the water tanks and sand boxes if necessary, making sure not to overfill the water tanks, as overflowing water drops down onto the loco's side rods and axle box lubricators, replacing some of the oil with water. The driver, having just finished oiling up, takes a very dim view of this, and will let the fireman know! In the meantime, the guard has cleared the line from Rinadeena and tells the driver he has the line to Teepookana.

RIGHT: Dubbil Barril on the King River, one of the most remote railway localities in Tasmania. In November 1962, an Abt loco hauls a rake of empties up the 1 in 20 rack towards Rinadeena. ~ Bernie Kelly

BELOW: Mount Lyell Railway tickets. ~ Galley Museum, Queenstown

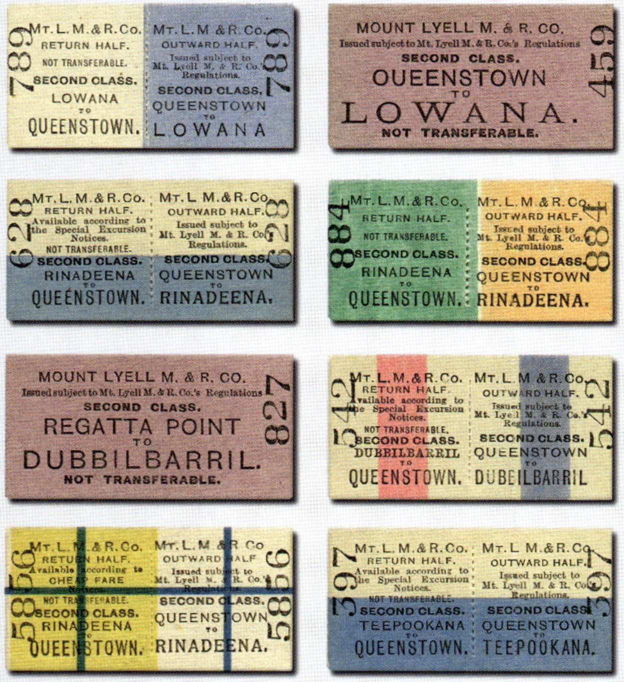

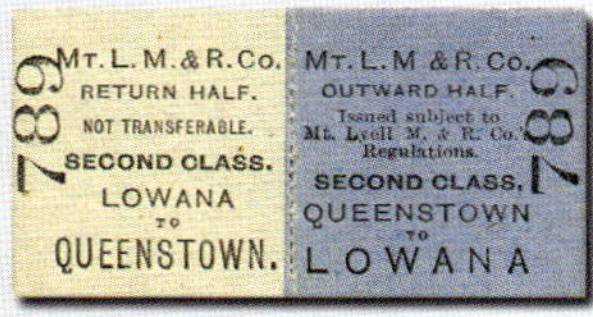

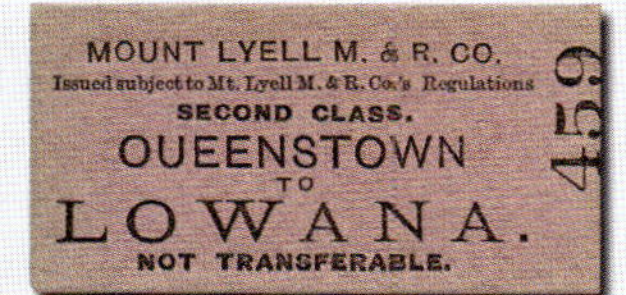

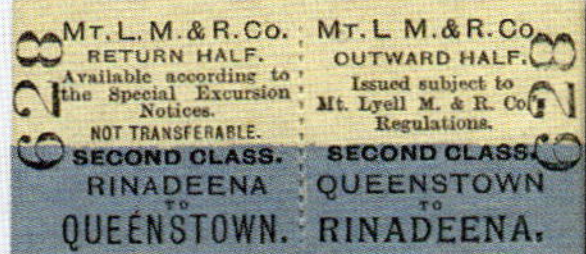

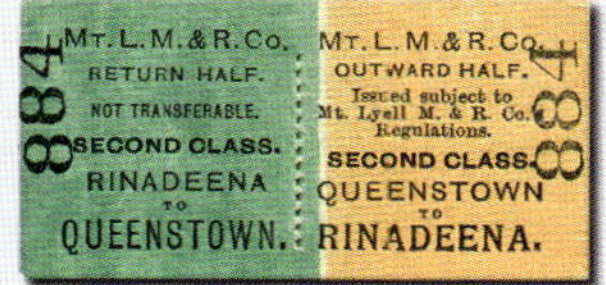

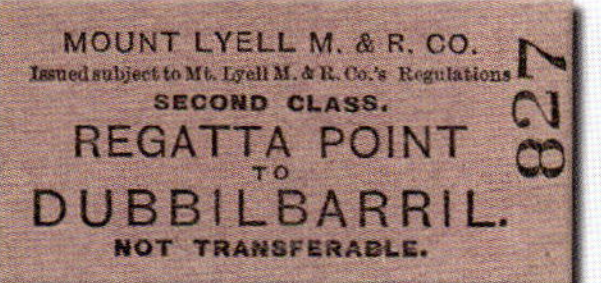

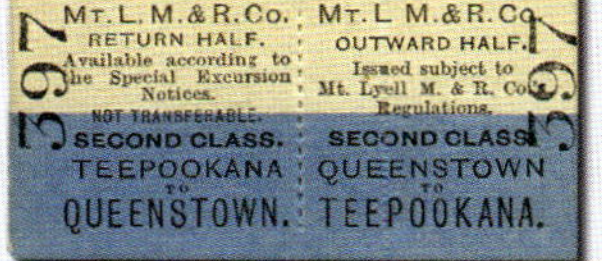

A dreary day at Regatta Point in the late 1950s. ~ Roy Busby, Train Hobby Publications

Crossing the Quarter Mile bridge in February 1960. ~ Keith Atkinson, Train Hobby Publications

The driver blows the whistle and the train steams out of Dubbil Barril. The run is fairly average on this section of the line, with a mixture of steaming and rolling, the exception being the Quarter Mile bridge, over which there is a speed limit of five mph. After crossing this bridge, there is a slight uphill pull, before the train rolls down into Teepookana.

From here, the train crosses the King River on an iron bridge, and then begins a pleasant flat run around the river's edge to Lowana, which like Teepookana is a small fettler settlement. The loco mainly coasts along this section, and isn't working too hard. A short stop is made at Lowana for the guard to get the line to Regatta Point. He advises the driver of this, and whether any empties need dropping off at the pyritic ore dump on the way. The driver steams off once again along the Lowana straight, around past Wesselman's farm to the approach of the 1 in 40 grade of the Letts Bay hill. By this time the driver has really got the old loco 'singing' to get a good run up this grade, and once over the top it is downhill to the ore dump. From here, the train rolls into the platform at Regatta Point station, where the passengers disembark after travelling on one of the greatest little railways in Australia.

REGATTA POINT

The loco is then uncoupled from the carriages and steamed over to the turntable to be turned for the return journey to Queenstown. A quick stop over the pit, and the usual routine of watering, checking and oiling begins. The fireman gives the gauge glasses a thorough 'blow through', to make sure they do not give a false reading. Then a little shunting takes place in the station yard, with the return train to Queenstown being made up. This normally consists of empty ore wagons, loaded coke wagons and the guard's van. The journey back to Queenstown is similar to the morning's run, with the exception being that two trips up the 1 in 20 rack section may be required to lift the load, half at a time.

DAY'S END

After arriving back at Queenstown, about an hour's shunting is required in the yard before the loco returns to the running shed. After bringing the loco to a halt in the shed, the driver shuts off the regulator, winds the reversing wheel into the centre position, then opens the rack and adhesion release cocks, closes the steam valve to the vacuum brake ejector, puts the hand brake on hard and finally opens the adhesion and rack exhaust columns. The fireman fills the boiler right up with water until the injectors kick off, then closes down the oil fire, fills the hydrostatic lubricator, and closes the firebox dampers. After shutting down the engine, the driver makes a report into the loco's maintenance book for any urgent work to be done by the fitters, and following this, the day's work is over for the engine crew, after another safe run over Tasmania's famous Abt railway.

THE MEN WHO MAINTAINED THE LOCOS

The sturdy little Abt locos ran for well over 60 years from 1896 to the line's closure in 1963, and were in quite good working condition when they retired. I put this down to the workers of the Mount Lyell Mining and Railway Company who took pride in their work and maintained them. From the foundry men who cast the bearings and other parts, to the turners who machined them and the boilermakers who made the new boilers, water tanks and fuel oil tanks, etc. Then there were the welders and fitters who put them back together, and not forgetting the drivers, firemen and cleaners. All these men did an excellent job, and were true tradesmen.

Mount Lyell Railway Engineman

Malcolm Powell

A Krauss 2 ft gauge loco hauls a 3 ft 6 in gauge coke wagon to the smelter over dual gauge track. 23 May 1963. ~ Weston Langford

Former engineman Malcolm Powell recalls his days working on the Mount Lyell Railway.

I began on the Mount Lyell railway in 1933 as an engine cleaner, and later progressed to fireman and then driver. In all, I spent 30 years on the Abt engines, before finishing up in 1963, just prior to the line closing. The Abt engines were coal fired when I began, and the fireman was kept pretty busy on the grade, shovelling lots of coal. But in later years the engines were converted to oil firing, which made things an awful lot easier for the fireman, although I never thought the engines steamed as well on oil.

In the earlier days the company used the Baldwin locos, which could only haul very small loads over the rack sections, or else they'd slip and slide. The Baldwins were mostly used at Regatta Point for shunting. In the latter years before the diesels arrived, the company had two DS steam engines. They never worked the rack, and were only allowed between Regatta Point and Dubbil Barril. The DS locos went well when they steamed, but they often wouldn't, and we had a lot of trouble with them, especially with the superheaters.

The Mount Lyell Company also had a 2 ft gauge system, with Krauss engines. These locos could haul six trucks out to the mine at Comstock, and you'd bring them back with fifteen tons of ore in each, a total of 90 tons. The grade on this track was so steep that it had two zig-zags. Trains were controlled with the vacuum brake, and these brakes gradually became weaker and weaker, but you knew when the train entered the next curve it would slow up. Then you could brake again, and this would be enough to get control of the train. When the rails were greasy, you'd look back and see the wheels just skidding along, so you'd put down sand, which gave you grip and assisted with braking, and soon enough you'd get the trucks under control.

We learned so much about controlling heavy trains on the Comstock line, which was tremendous grounding for when we got out and drove trains on the mainline.

In February 1960, a 2 ft gauge Krauss loco shunts coke wagons on dual gauge track. ~ Keith Atkinson, Train Hobby Publications

A West Coast Childhood

VIV CROCKER

Queenstown born and bred, Viv Crocker has been involved with the Mount Lyell Mining and Railway Company his whole life. As a child he rode the trains, then as an adult he worked on the mines as an electrical fitter, and in later years he was heavily involved in the Abt railway rebuilding effort. Now, at age 80, Viv retains fascinating memories of Queenstown and its railway in their glory days.

QUEENSTOWN

My mother, one of eight children, arrived at Strahan in 1888. Her father was a bee keeper from Triabunna on Tasmania's East Coast, and he had been finding things pretty tough, so he decided to head west. My father came from Beechworth in Victoria. Times were tough there too, so in 1903 he headed over to Tasmania with a couple of mates, looking for work. He intended to stay for three months but ended up staying for the rest of his life! My parents raised seven children, of which I am the youngest. Dad worked for the Mount Lyell Company for many years – employment which suited him well, as it was very secure. He died in Queenstown at the age of 94.

As kids of the West Coast, we occupied our time very nicely. We roamed around the hills, we went prospecting, we rode on the train, and we went to Strahan for our holidays, which was just part and parcel of life in the hills. Strahan Picnic Day was the highlight of the year for Queenstown's kids. The Company put on trains of C class trucks, which normally hauled coke, and they rigged up canvas roofs and seats, and these carried great numbers of picnickers to Strahan and back. Four of these trains headed off to Strahan in the morning and came back in the afternoon. The kids loved hanging out of the trains and grabbing hold of a few ferns on the way, and on the rack section, they jumped out and ran ahead – so slow was the pace – picking a bunch of flowers for mum before jumping back in the carriage.

One of the other great things for the kids in Queenstown was the left over bits of copper to be found. These copper nodules, about the size of marbles, fell off the railway trucks during transit, so on Sundays we'd go scrounging along the railway to pick them up and use in our shanghais.

Abt loco No. 2 at Queenstown, January 1961.
~ Keith Atkinson, Train Hobby Publications

Looking up Orr Street, Queenstown, in January 1953. The denuded slopes of Mount Owen form an imposing backdrop. ~ Peter Ralph

WORKING FOR THE MOUNT LYELL COMPANY

I attended the high school at Queenstown, but it came to the point where if I wanted to continue my education, it meant moving to either Hobart or Launceston. I didn't want to impose this expense on my parents, who'd already raised six kids before me, so in 1951 I took an apprenticeship at the Mount Lyell Mining and Railway Company as an electrical fitter.

I had a very good life working for the company, and even though I had a few breaks over the years, doing other work around the town, I always went back. Being with the Mount Lyell Company meant working on a huge variety of equipment and installations. We worked on all the above-ground equipment, as well as underground installations, and I also used to re-wind the armatures on the English Electric locomotives which operated the underground railway system. These locomotives hauled 75 tons of ore through the horizontal tunnels, and they were magnificent.

I also had the pleasure, or sometimes lack thereof, of travelling on the Mount Lyell trains as a commuter, which was just part of the work scene in those days.

I finished up in charge of the electrical department at Mount Lyell, and I had a fairly large budget and about 70 people working for me – a great responsibility. I held this position until 1989, when the company was talking of selling the mine, and I took retrenchment at the age of 55.

ABOVE: A 2 ft gauge electric loco at Mount Lyell works. February 1960. ~ Keith Atkinson, Train Hobby Publications

RIGHT: Pouring copper anodes at the Mount Lyell smelter in April 1957. ~ Peter Ralph

The view over bustling Queenstown, as it was in April 1957. In the background is the imposing hulk of Mount Owen, while in the foreground is 'Penghana', the luxurious abode of Mount Lyell Mining and Railway Company General Manager Robert Sticht. Following his appointment as General Manager, Sticht built the grand mansion, which had commanding views over the town. After having part of the intervening hillside blasted away, Sticht was able to sit on Penghana's balcony and observe the Mount Lyell smelter in operation! ~ Peter Ralph

MORE THAN JUST A RAILWAY

The Mount Lyell Railway was far more than just an industrial line that ran from point A to point B – it was a very important part of the town's life – and it had tremendous character and romance attached to it. It was a real family line. Fettlers and line maintenance people, along with their families, lived at the remote intermediate stations along the line, such as Teepookana, Rinadeena and Dubbil Barril. There were about sixteen of these railway families, and they lived in pretty harsh, isolated sorts of conditions. All their food was ordered from Queenstown and was carried in the guard's van. When the train approached one of these remote houses along the way, it would slow down to allow the guard to jump off and deliver the bread and milk, or a meat order. The company allowed the workers along the line to use trolleys to gather their firewood. They'd roll them up the track, load them with firewood, then release the brakes and let them roll back down the hill to the house. Many of the people along the line raised cattle for a supply of milk, and milk cans were picked up and taken into Queenstown on the train. Every day people queued up at Queenstown station waiting for the train to come in, to pick up their milk and other goods.

Queenstown residents jumped on the train to go on a picnic, or to visit friends or relatives in Strahan. We used it very much like a city person might take a tram or a bus to go to the beach. The O class passenger carriages were clerestory roofed stock, and were introduced in 1902. In their day, they were considered to be amongst the most luxurious carriages in Australia. They came complete with leather seats, and had brass fittings and coat hangers, as well as sliding windows. The company had lots of rolling stock in these years, with both steam and diesel locomotives, and the railway was managed very competently.

LIKE A SUBURB OF MELBOURNE

Up until 1932 when the road from Hobart was put through, every single morsel of food and clothing, along with the mining equipment, etc, all came into town on the train. The produce of the mine was railed out, and the townspeople always used the train whenever they went out of town. In actual fact the railway was an artery between Queenstown and Melbourne, rather than anywhere else. The Mount Lyell Company headquarters was in Melbourne, and because Queenstown was isolated from the rest of Tasmania, the town was effectively like a suburb of Melbourne. Steamships regularly came and went across Bass Strait, delivering the latest fashions and luxuries from Collins Street boutiques, along with produce, beer and Melbourne newspapers – in fact, Queenstown probably received *The Sun* newspaper before Hobart did! West Coast residents ardently followed Melbourne football clubs in the Victorian Football League, and most people who went on holidays or on their honeymoon ventured to Melbourne.

The West Coast is noted for its treacherous, wild weather, and at times the Mount Lyell line had to be closed while landslides were cleared. Surprisingly, no major accidents were ever recorded in the history of the line, although on one lucky occasion part of a bridge collapsed just as a train had passed over it. One of the most impressive structures along the railway was the magnificent, curved Quarter Mile bridge over the King River, which had a severe speed limit. The drivers barely cracked the regulator when they passed over this rickety bridge, and you could really feel the lateral swaying movement when the train went across.

The locos were coal-fired until the late 1950s when they were converted to oil firing. This was due to the ever increasing cost of importing good quality steaming coal. Oil firing reduced costs, but some of the crews thought the engines were never the same, and the oil was certainly a lot dirtier than coal. Coal firing had its problems, with many sparks being shot out of the funnel, particularly when the train was hauling a big load. These sparks caused fires on occasions, and they were a particular problem on the rack section between Dubbil Barril and Rinadeena, where there were thirteen timber trestle bridges. Every one of these bridges had a 44 gallon drum placed at its base, to be used for fire fighting purposes. If a spark ignited one of the bridges, the engine crew or guard of the following train pulled up, and they extinguished the flames using a bucket and water from these drums. There was certainly nothing complex about this system, but it worked!

A BUSY LINE

In the busy years, the line had up to six trains running on some days – 5 am, 6 am, 7 am, 7.45 am, 10 am and then the midday train. The first train of a morning normally took 120 tons of copper or other products from the mine to Strahan. Only 60 tons could be hauled up the rack, so the train stopped at Halls Creek, near the bottom of the incline. There, two trucks were disconnected and placed in the siding. The following train then hooked on and pushed from behind, and they'd separate at Rinadeena, at the top of the grade, where the first loco would head back down to Halls Creek to pick up the remaining wagons. So these two trains would, between them, shuttle the whole consist up the rack section. This constant

The manager's car climbs the rack in 1957. ~ Frank Kelly, Bernie Kelly collection

shuttling of small loads up and down the rack went on all day. The pushing loco was never attached, and was not only used for traction, but also as a safety device in case the front loco lost traction. The 7.45 am was known as the 'through' train, and was generally used as the commuter train. The 'through' took 2½ hours to run from Queenstown to Regatta Point, where it arrived at 10.15 am.

A new suburb, called Hurst Street, was built in Queenstown by the mining company, and it was pretty close to the railway line. It consisted of about 30 houses, and after some time there were over 100 children of various ages in this new suburb – an average of about four or five kids per house. After a few years, people began to notice the many small children running around, and wondered what might be causing the high birth rate. It seemed that the cause was not of a medical nature, but simply due to the 5 o'clock train which came through every morning. Some of the drivers used the whistle somewhat 'over-zealously' for the two nearby road crossings. Many of the residents were rudely woken by the whistling, and at that ungodly hour, it was too late to get back to sleep, but too early to get up, so there was only one thing left to do....

CLOSURE

In the early 1960s, the Tasmanian Government finally decided to spend a bit of money on the West Coast roads, which allowed trucks into Queenstown. This situation pleased many people, but it also resulted in the Abt line being threatened with closure. This news caused quite a groundswell of support to keep the line open for tourists, although in those days, tourism to the West Coast was in its infancy. In fact visitors were almost regarded by the company as being a bit of a nuisance – the attitude at times was, 'Ah, we'll have to put on an extra carriage for them.' Visitors who travelled on the railway were really taken with it, with its unique Abt rack system and magnificent gorge scenery, and the line was quite a tourist drawcard. But the cost to keep the line open was enormous, so in 1963 the railway was closed, and it was sadly missed!

ABT RAILWAY CHILD

JUDY CROCKER

I certainly enjoyed being an Abt 'railway child', although as kids, of course, we really didn't know any other style of life. My father came to Queenstown from Waratah, further up the West Coast, in search of work. He was an outdoors sort of man, and he picked up a job as a fettler on the Abt railway. He married, and my parents raised two boys and two girls.

We lived for a while at Rinadeena, at the top of the rack section. Rinadeena is from the Aboriginal dialect and means, 'A drop of rain', which is a bit of an understatement! We then lived at Lynchford, which was named after the famous Irish rebel, Con Lynch. The families who lived along the line visited each other regularly, and shared a great communal spirit. Sometimes our family would travel into Queenstown on 'Pay Friday' on the rail motor, and on Saturday nights we occasionally used the ganger's trolley to come into Queenstown and go to the movies, knowing there wouldn't be any trains on the line. Us kids rode a bike to and from school, about four miles each way, and thought nothing of it. Things were a bit tough in those times, but we made the most of it – I loved living on the railway in all weather and in all the elements.

The train drivers were very friendly towards the kids, and they threw newspapers and other things out to us. One trick was for the dads to send the kids outside as the train passed to pull faces at the engine crew, with the hope that one of them would throw a lump of coal at us cheeky kids. Then dad would come out with the shovel and add the lump to the rest of the company's coal, to be used in the fire!

On Saturdays, dad used to put me on the afternoon train at Lynchford. I'd go into Queenstown to pick up the bread and the family 'brick' of ice cream, wrapped in newspaper, along with other treats. Then I'd have to pedal back home – the road from Queenstown to Lynchford was in terribly poor condition – even taxis wouldn't go near it, it was so rough! So if you wanted to get around, you either rode your bike, or else it was 'shank's pony'.

LATER YEARS

In 1953, a turntable was installed at Dubbil Barril in order to turn both the Abt locos and the Drewry diesels, which arrived on the railway in that year. As traffic increased, the Abt locos were used mainly on the rack sections, with the diesels used on the flat section between Dubbil Barril and Regatta Point. Also in the 1950s, a large pyrite and coke handling facility was built near Regatta Point, and a little Ruston diesel locomotive, nicknamed 'Flossy', was used to shunt the adjacent yard. The coke was imported for use in the Mount Lyell smelter, while the pyrites were exported for use in the fertiliser manufacturing industry.

In its latter years, the Mount Lyell Railway became something of a tourist drawcard, due to the unique Abt system and wonderful mountain scenery along its 22 mile route. A lack of proper roads on the West Coast elevated the railway's importance, but by the 1960s, this situation was beginning to change. Queenstown had been connected by road to Hobart only in 1932, but recent upgrades to roads linking Queenstown to Strahan and Zeehan raised the possibility of road transport taking over from rail. The line had become more and more expensive to maintain, particularly the many bridges, and in October 1962 the company announced that the railway would close.

The final passenger train ran on the line on 29 June 1963. A large crowd attended the departure of the train from Queenstown in a touching ceremony, and more than a few tears were shed, as a way of life drew to a close. It was a sad day for railwaymen and residents alike, as many locals had developed a great affection for the little train. People reasoned that the line should be retained as a tourist attraction, but the Mount Lyell Company was unmoved, and before long, trucks laden with Mount Lyell copper began lumbering along the road to Strahan. On 10 August 1963, the last goods train pulled into Queenstown yard, and the old Mount Lyell Railway was no more.

RIGHT: Surrounded by well-wishers, the last passenger train to run on the Mount Lyell Railway prepares to depart Queenstown station on 29 June 1963. ~ Michael Schrader, Train Hobby Publications

LABOR
OMNIA
VINCIT
WE FIND A WAY
OR MAKE IT

ABOVE: The last passenger train at Queenstown on 29 June 1963.
~ Michael Schrader, Train Hobby Publications

LEFT: The last passenger train arrives at Regatta Point on 29 June 1963. The shield on Abt No.1 loco's smokebox – a replica of that used on the line's grand opening back in 1897 – proclaims in Latin, 'Labor Omnia Vincit' – 'We Find a Way or Make It'.
~ Keith Atkinson, Train Hobby Publications

Lake Margaret Power Station and Tramway

An enormous quantity of firewood was consumed annually by the Mount Lyell Company, with timber being used for mining supports, building material and as fuel for the smelters, at a rate of hundreds of tons per week. Before long, the hillsides surrounding Queenstown were stripped bare, and with tramways being extended into outlaying areas, an army of timber cutters cut a swath through the forests at an ever increasing cost. Coal was used on a limited basis, but it was very expensive, so in 1911 hydro-electricity was considered as an alternate source of energy. Lake Margaret, five miles to the north of Queenstown, was selected as the site for a power station, and work commenced in 1912. A 2 ft gauge steel railed tramway was built to link Queenstown with Lake Margaret. A wooden pipeline from the lake to the power station was built using Canadian Douglas Fir, and an inspection tramway was built alongside.

In all, the project cost £164,000, and the first transmission of power occurred in November 1914. It was estimated that electricity from the Lake Margaret power station saved the Mount Lyell mine £50,000 in its first year of operation, and the project put an end to the large scale firewood industry of Queenstown, with an estimated 1,300,000 tons of firewood having been consumed over the previous twenty years. In the following decades, further turbines were added, then later an entire additional power station.

Following construction, the tramway continued to provide a service for the families living at the little village at Lake Margaret – its only access to the outside world. Motive power on the tram consisted of a Krauss steam locomotive, which was later replaced by an Nicola Romeo petrol loco. Regular services included the Wednesday shopping train, and Saturday night social runs, which allowed people to enjoy a night out in Queenstown. School children were transported to and from Queenstown in a Vauxhall rail motor. The Lake Margaret Tramway ceased operating in 1964, when a road was constructed.

The Lake Margaret power station supplied all the Mount Lyell electricity needs until the late 1940s. The pipeline was replaced in 1938 with King Billy Pine, and this material lasted until the power station closed in mid July 2006. In 2009, the pipeline was rebuilt using Alaskan Yellow Cedar. The power station was reopened in that year, and continues to supply a large percentage of the mine's power requirements to this day.

ABOVE: Nicola Romeo petrol shunter at Lake Margaret. November 1962.
~ Bernie Kelly

RIGHT: The Lake Margaret Tramway in full flight! The Vauxhall rail motor zips along the 2 ft gauge track. January 1963.
~ Keith Atkinson, Train Hobby Publications

The West Coast Today

Claimed by the forest. A rotting North Lyell Railway wagon at Pillinger, 90 years after the railway ceased operating. ~ Nick Anchen

A wondrous array of adventures and fascinating industrial archaeology await the keen historian and lover of wild places on Tasmania's West Coast. History can be re-lived with a steam train ride on the West Coast Wilderness Railway or the Wee Georgie Wood Steam Railway, and many relics of the railway age are accessible by foot, bicycle or 4WD, so long as mud, obnoxious weather, abundant leeches and the odd snake are not too much of a deterrent!

EMU BAY RAILWAY

Today, 136 years after horses began hauling tin from the Mount Bischoff mine to the Emu Bay wharf, trains still grace the rails of the grand old Emu Bay Railway. Trains currently operate on 130 km of track between Burnie and the Melba Flats loading facility. South of Melba Flats, much of the eight kilometres of abandoned track remains in place, and can be followed in parts through to the outskirts of Zeehan. The iron bridge which carried the rails across the North East Dundas Tramway remains in position.

From Guildford, the dismantled ten mile spur to Waratah, which last saw train services in 1940, can be traced in places, and the old iron railway bridge remains over a lake at Waratah, just short of the former terminus. The scattered ruins of the old Mount Bischoff tin mine workings – previously accessible – are currently off limits, due to rehabilitation works being carried out.

Steam and diesel excursion trains were once a regular feature on the EBR, but tragically, these popular rail adventures have been disallowed in recent years. Should this unfortunate situation be reversed, a journey along this most scenic railway is not to be missed!

ZEEHAN

The former Zeehan-Strahan railway, operated by the Tasmanian Government Railways between 1892 and 1960, was mostly obliterated in the 1960s, thanks to a paved road being built over the former right-of-way. A short section of gently winding railway formation, adjacent to the main road, can easily be driven along. The former station and yard at West Strahan have suffered the indignity of having a caravan park built on them, but the highlight of the old Government line is the Strahan to Regatta Point section, a delightful 3 km walking track following the old railway around the water's edge, with scenic views of Macquarie Harbour.

At Zeehan, an interesting rail trail extends 6 km to the old Comstock mine, following the route of several former tramways. Of particular interest is the spray tunnel, which can be driven through with a small car.

WARATAH

It is possible to explore the route of the Magnet Tramway, which operated between 1901 and 1940. The old formation is now a muddy 4WD track, running through lush forested country, with detours around the old decaying bridges. The trail is accessed from the rubbish tip off Waratah Road, south west of Waratah township, and runs for 10 km to the interesting Magnet mine ruins.

The famous tin mining town of Waratah, pictured in 1956. In the foreground next to Waratah Falls are the crumbling ore dressing sheds, which processed tin from Mount Bischoff's highly profitable mine. Visible in the background is the iron Emu Bay Railway bridge. ~ Peter Ralph

WEE GEORGIE WOOD STEAM RAILWAY

Wee Georgie Wood gleams in glorious afternoon sunshine at Tullah. February 1998. ~ Peter Ralph

The North Mount Farrell Tramway closed in 1964, and today no trace of the tramway is identifiable at Farrell Junction. Much of the formation has vanished under the murky waters of Lake Rosebery, although a short section remains visible when water levels allow. Happily, at the Tullah end, tourist trains operate on a fun 2 km trip, part of which follows the original North Mount Farrell Tramway route.

When the tramway closed, the diminutive and rather famous loco, *Wee Georgie Wood*, was saved from the scrap yard by indignant Tullah locals, and preserved on static display. Then in 1977, a group called the Wee Georgie Wood Steam Railway Inc. was formed to keep the spirit of the old North Mount Farrell Tramway alive. The group, a collection of locals and railway enthusiasts from other parts of Tasmania, began the task of restoring the engine to its former glory, then building nearly 2 km of track in Tullah. The grand reopening took place on 5 February 1987.

A passenger carriage, formerly used on the Lake Margaret Tramway near Queenstown, was lovingly restored and is used to carry passengers, and the former Lake Margaret Tramway Nicola Romeo petrol mechanical loco of 1925, has also been restored and hauls trains when *Wee Georgie Wood* is out of action for repairs. Subsequently, a loco shed and passenger station have been built, and the enterprising group has plans for the future, which include the restoration of Krauss loco No.9 – a former veteran of the tramway – and additional passenger carriages, along with a proposed extension of the track.

Since reopening, the little train has become a tourist favourite – particularly with children – as the tiny engine and carriages have a 'toy train' appearance. A ride behind *Wee Georgie Wood* is a fun and very casual affair, with the little engine galloping along the 2 ft gauge track through the picturesque township of Tullah, with Mount Murchison looming large in the distance.

Taking water at Tullah. February 1998. ~ Peter Ralph

Wee Georgie Wood thunders along the track! ~ Peter Ralph

West Coast Wilderness Railway

Abt loco No. 5, bathed in winter sunshine at Rinadeena in June 2007. ~ Tony 'Ashcat' Marsden

The closure of the Mount Lyell Railway in 1963 caused much sadness for many residents, particularly in Queenstown, where the railway had been a significant part of the town's fabric for over 60 years. The Mount Lyell Railway, often simply called the Abt Railway, was seen by some as a golden tourism opportunity. Various ideas and proposals were put forward through the years and decades following its dismantling, but the funding was never available, and the proposals all came to naught.

Meanwhile, the West Coast climate took its toll, and with the bridges rapidly decaying and the formation becoming overgrown with dense vegetation, any possibility of the railway being rebuilt seemed less and less likely.

ABOVE: Old telegraph pole near Teepookana. ~ Nick Anchen

ABOVE RIGHT: The sad remains of the old Quarter Mile bridge, a once-grand structure which has been claimed by the ravages of time, along with successive King River floods. ~ Peter Ralph

RIGHT: Deep in the rainforest at Camp Spur, a rusting section of Abt system test track remains in place. ~ Nick Anchen

THE ABT RAILWAY SOCIETY

VIV CROCKER

In the mid 1990s, Queenstown resident Viv Crocker, a former employee of the Mount Lyell Company, led a new movement to rebuild the Abt railway.

In 1994, Renison Goldfields Consolidated, as the Mount Lyell company was then officially called, announced that the copper mine would close. This was of great concern for Queenstown, one of Australia's last remaining historic mining towns, as the population of 3,500 was very dependent on the mines, and closure would have been disastrous. I found myself a bit bored in retirement, so I became part of the thrust to rebuild and reopen the railway. My wife and four sons were also involved. Judy, being one of the original railway kids, certainly knew the importance of the railway.

The idea to rebuild the line really struck a chord. The thinking was that the project could employ many of the locals – designers, draughtsmen, engineers, tradesmen and artisans. This proposal generated an enormous amount of interest, and we called public meetings. The first of these meetings was on a cold night in Queenstown, and when it began we had the grand total of six people in the room. I thought, oh, this is going to be the greatest flop ever, but within a few minutes, we had about 75 people present, and the 'Abt Railway Society' was born!

We were told we were dreaming, and in truth we were. A core of about eight people began the task, and we soon developed a tremendous respect for the men who built the line back in the 1890s! We raised funds and attracted publicity. We had costing done, and the estimate to rebuild the railway was put at about $19 million – a figure which included helping to clean up the environmental disaster that was the King River. Soon, we obtained a government grant, which enabled us to employ some young people to clear the overgrown formation from Queenstown to Rinadeena. We put in drainage, and suddenly for the first time in many years, the formation became dry. Then we organised an open day, with film crews and so on turning up, and the press reacted positively. This media attention resulted in certain politicians suddenly becoming interested in what we were doing, whereas before these same people had told us we were mad, and asked us what we had been smoking!

The line had 40 bridges which needed rebuilding, and this obstacle was the main point for the many detractors. People kept asking us, 'How will you rebuild all those bridges?' Luckily, bridge building technology had come a long way since the line was built in the 1890s. The society applied for Federation Funding, and in July 1998, the Federal Government announced a $20.45 million grant to rebuild the line. This was wonderful news, but it was only the start. The real challenge now began – reconstruction of the railway, and making the best use of taxpayer dollars.

A DAUNTING PROSPECT

Following funding approval, work commenced on the mammoth Abt railway rebuilding effort – a huge undertaking. After nearly four decades of neglect, the formation was overgrown and in places covered with landslips. All of the timber bridges were completely rotten and in need of replacement. In the end, 39 bridges would be constructed along the 35 km route. The project began in earnest in late 1999.

One of the main obstacles was the crossing of the King River at two points – first the Quarter Mile bridge, in a remote and inaccessible valley between Dubbil Barril and Teepookana. The old bridge had long since collapsed, and its replacement was far shorter, at just 90 metres, built on a new alignment with Bailey bridge panels. At Teepookana, the old iron bridge spanning the King was found to be salvageable, and was reconditioned.

Track laying began in May 2000. In January 2001, fully restored Abt No. 3 locomotive arrived at Queenstown, and within weeks, train running commenced. Former Mount Lyell Railway driver Malcolm Powell, by then in his 80s, was given the honour of driving the first train since 1963 up the 1 in 16 rack section to Rinadeena. Finally on 27 December 2002, the first passenger train ran right through from Queenstown to Regatta Point.

The line was officially opened on 3 April 2003 by the Prime Minister, John Howard, and the Tasmanian Premier, Jim Bacon. In all, restoration had taken a little over three years – a remarkable achievement – at a total cost of over $30 million, which included a mixture of federal, state and private funding.

ABOVE: Abt No. 3 taking water at Rinadeena in 2004. ~ Peter Ralph

RIGHT: In late afternoon sunshine, Abt No. 1 heads for the engine shed at Queenstown, after a hard day's work out on the track. 16 February 2006. ~ Nick Anchen

The West Coast Wilderness Railway workshops at Queenstown in March 2013. Abt No. 5 is on the left, awaiting the refitting of its driving wheel assembly (seen in the foreground), and Abt No. 3 is on the right. ~ Nick Anchen

With four of the five original Abt locomotives having been preserved when the Mount Lyell Railway closed in 1963, it was only natural that they would feature in the restoration plans. Abt No.1, which had resided at the Zeehan Pioneers Museum, and Abt No.3, which had been on display at the Miner's Siding monument at Queenstown, were selected for restoration. The two engines underwent complete rebuilds, including brand new boilers, at Saunders and Ward Company in Kingston, Tasmania. Abt No.3 was delivered to Queenstown in January 2001 and Abt No.1 arrived in September 2001.

The two original Mount Lyell Railway Vulcan Drewry diesel mechanical locomotives were also obtained, and were used extensively on construction trains. Once train running commenced, the diesels were utilised on the lower section of the line, running daily tourist trains between Regatta Point and Dubbil Barril.

Once it was recognised that two Abt locos were insufficient, additional motive power was sought. Abt No.5 had been on display at the Puffing Billy Railway in Victoria since the 1960s, and in November 2003 it was repatriated to Tasmania. After a full restoration, it re-entered traffic on the West Coast Wilderness Railway in August 2005.

In the 1960s, the Mount Lyell Railway O class passenger carriages had been sold to the Puffing Billy Railway in Victoria, where they were regauged to 2 ft 6 in and are used to this day as first class dining cars. An entire new carriage fleet was built for use on the new railway, with ten passenger cars and one kitchen car currently in service.

ABOVE: Vulcan Drewry diesel mechanical locomotives, D1 and D2, at Regatta Point station in 2004. ~ Peter Ralph

RIGHT: Name and builder's plates of diesel locomotive D2, *Mount Lyell*. ~ Nick Anchen

A Journey on the West Coast Wilderness Railway

MOUNT LYELL No 1

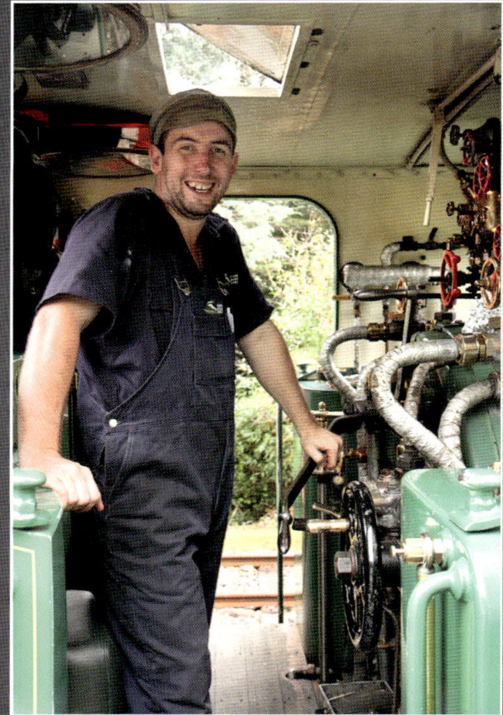

Driver James Smith on the footplate of his beloved engine, Abt No. 1.

Abt No.1 standing outside the Queenstown shed, prior to running to Dubbil Barril. 16 March 2013. ~ All images Nick Anchen

Fireman Allie Hume, taking water during the short stop at Lynchford.

W.C.W.R
psi

Lake Margaret Power Station

Little remains to be seen of the former Lake Margaret Tramway, but the Lake Margaret power station and pipeline area is worth exploring.

This facility dates back to 1914 and was built to power the Mount Lyell mine, replacing the unsustainable consumption of firewood. The power station still functions, as does the re-built timber pipeline and adjacent timber-railed inspection tramway, both of which lead to Lake Margaret. Access to the site is via a gravel road off the main Zeehan Highway, some 10 km north of Queenstown.

On a visit by the author in February 2006, the 70 year old King Billy pipeline was well and truly past its use-by date. It was leaking spectacularly, making the scenic 3 km walk to the dam wall at Lake Margaret an exhilarating if drenching experience! ~ All images Nick Anchen

North East Dundas Tramway Remains

The former North East Dundas Tramway route can easily be accessed via a superb 5 km walking track from the now-defunct township of Williamsford, near Rosebery. The twisting formation still retains rotting timber bridges and many old sleepers, some with dog spikes intact. The walk culminates at the spectacular Montezuma Falls, the tallest cascade in Tasmania.

After crossing the gully on a steel bridge, the track runs for a further 14 km to a point on the Murchison Highway near Melba Flats railway terminus. The going here is much rougher and can be quite muddy at times, but is accessible by 4WD vehicle.

All in all, this exhilarating tramp is almost indescribably beautiful, and the greatest example of a former railway in Tasmania – possibly Australia. In addition to the railway, the Hercules haulage at Williamsford and the rusting 1929 vintage aerial cableway, used to transport ore to Rosebery, are both very much in evidence.
~ All images Nick Anchen

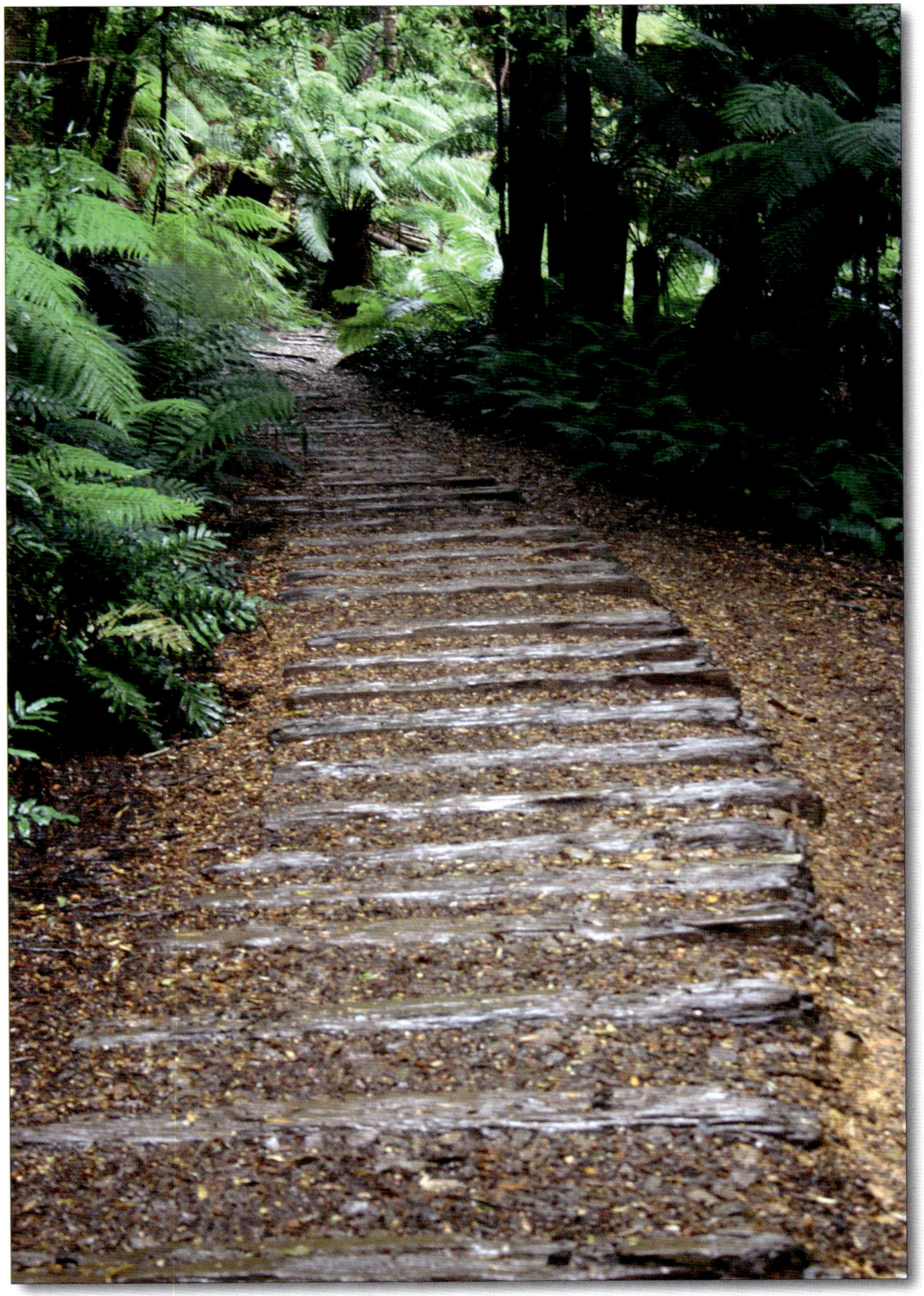

Mount Lyell and Queenstown

At Mount Lyell, mining operations still linger on, although at a much reduced scale compared to the boom years. In its first century of operations until temporary closure in 1994, 108 million tons of ore, yielding a total of 1.27 million tons of copper, along with 24 million ounces of silver, and 1.4 million ounces of gold, was extracted from the Mount Lyell mine. Although the vegetation is growing back, the lunar-like landscape of Queenstown's hills, combined with the stained Queen River, provide a striking reminder of the destructive mining methods of yesteryear.

A sense of history is to be found just over the hill from Queenstown, in the former bustling mining towns of Gormanston and Linda. This little-inhabited valley contains a scattering of ancient dwellings, most in a state of disrepair. From high up on the slopes of Mount Lyell, spectacular views are to be had in all directions, with the remains of railways and tramways visible criss-crossing the rocky scrub country above Linda. Also visible from this ridge is the flooded remains of the Iron Blow pit – a silent reminder of past endeavours.

LEFT and BELOW: Majestic lighting displays on a stormy afternoon atop Mount Lyell.
~ Both images Nick Anchen

The famous Iron Blow – the birthplace of the Mount Lyell copper field. This open cut pit was worked between 1886 and 1922. ~ Nick Anchen

North Lyell Railway Remains

Following the abandonment of the North Lyell Railway in the mid-1920s, this large iron bridge over the King River was used by road vehicles. Then in the 1990s, it was swallowed whole by the waters of newly created Lake Burbury, never to be seen again. March 1967. ~ Keith Atkinson, Train Hobby Publications

Exploring the remains of the old North Lyell Railway is an outstanding experience – indeed one of the highlight of a visit to the wilds of western Tasmania.

From Queenstown, a very scenic road leads south past the imposing Mount Jukes and Lake Burbury, from where the road traverses the old formation of the North Mount Lyell Railway, a line which last saw trains in the mid 1920s. This all-weather road continues on to the Franklin-Gordon Wild Rivers National Park, but a muddy track, (which could be considered strictly 4WD after heavy rain) swings south and continues to follow the railway formation. This 5 km track passes through spectacular scenery with impossibly deep cuttings as far as the Bird River bridge, beyond which vehicles are not permitted.

From this bridge, a magnificent if fairly rough 5 km trek follows the Bird River through lush rainforest to Kelly Basin, and the dark, mysterious waters of Macquarie Harbour. Kelly Basin is full of history – a rotting guard's van in amongst the tree ferns, remains of the extensive former brickworks, and the old jetty are all in evidence. A further scramble around the harbour through rough, swampy country, leads the explorer to remote Pillinger, where rusting rolling stock stands defiantly on equally rusty rails in a most fascinating setting.

Old boiler at Kelly Basin. ~ All images Nick Anchen

'Reindeer Lodge' fisherman's shack, partially built from an old guard's van.

Rotting wagon at Pillinger.

The deteriorating remains of a North Lyell Railway guard's van at Kelly Basin.

The rotting remains of Pillinger's once-thriving wharf area. In the tranquillity of Macquarie Harbour, with only the breeze in the tree tops and the occasional bird call to break the silence, it is difficult to imagine the bustling scenes of a century ago. ~ Nick Anchen